WHAT SAINT PAUL
REALLY SAID

For Keith Sutton

WHAT SAINT PAUL REALLY SAID

N. T. WRIGHT

WAS PAUL OF TARSUS THE REAL FOUNDER OF CHRISTIANITY?

WILLIAM B. EERDMANS PUBLISHING COMPANY
GRAND RAPIDS, MICHIGAN

FORWARD MOVEMENT PUBLICATIONS
CINCINNATI, OHIO

First published 1997 in the U.K. by
Lion Publishing plc
Sandy Lane West, Oxford, England
ISBN 0 7459 3797 7
Albatross Books Pty Ltd
PO Box 320, Sutherland, NSW 2232, Australia
ISBN 0 7324 1648 5

This edition published jointly 1997 in the United States of America by
Wm. B. Eerdmans Publishing Company
255 Jefferson Ave. S.E., Grand Rapids, Michigan 49503
and by
Forward Movement Publications
412 Sycamore Street, Cincinnati, Ohio 45202

Printed in the United States of America

09 08 07 06 05 04   14 13 12 11 10 9

Library of Congress Cataloging-in-Publication Data

Wright, N. T. (Nicholas Thomas)
      What Saint Paul really said: was Paul of Tarsus the real
  founder of Christianity? / by Tom Wright.
          p.   cm.
      Based on various lectures given at various places and times.
      Includes bibliographical references.
      Eerdmans ISBN 0-8028-4445-6 (pbk.: alk. paper)
      Forward Movement ISBN 0-88028-181-2
      1. Bible. N.T. Epistles of Paul—Theology. 2. Paul, the
  Apostle, Saint. 3. Christianity—Origin.   I. Title.
  BS2651.W75   1997
  225.9′2—dc21   97-8588
                                            CIP

Contents

Preface

Paul has provoked people as much in the twentieth century as he did in the first. Then, they sometimes threw stones at him; now, they tend to throw words. Some people still regard Paul as a pestilent and dangerous fellow. Others still think him the greatest teacher of Christianity after the Master himself. This spectrum of opinion is well represented in the scholarly literature as well as the popular mind.

I have lived with St Paul as a more or less constant companion for more than twenty years. Having written a doctoral dissertation on the letter to the Romans, a commentary on the letters to the Colossians and to Philemon, and a monograph on Paul's view of Christ and the law – not to mention several articles on various passages and themes within Paul's writings – I still have the sense of being only half-way up the mountain, of there being yet more to explore, more vistas to glimpse. Often (not always), when I read what other scholars say about Paul, I have the feeling of looking downwards into the mist, rather than upwards to the mountain-top. Always I am aware that I myself have a good deal more climbing yet to do.

The present book is therefore something of an interim report, and an incomplete one at that. My large volume, in which I hope to do for Paul what I have tried to do for Jesus in *Jesus and the Victory of God* (SPCK and Fortress, 1996), is still in preparation. But I have lectured on certain aspects of Paul's thinking in various places over the last few years, and several of those who heard the lectures have encouraged me to make them available to a wider audience. I am very grateful for the invitations to give the Selwyn Lectures in Lichfield Cathedral, the Gheens Lectures at Southern Baptist Theological Seminary in Louisville, Kentucky, the Prideaux Lectures at Exeter University, and some guest lectures at Asbury Seminary, Kentucky and at the Canadian Theological Seminary in Regina, Saskatchewan. My hosts were enormously hospitable, my audiences enthusiastic, and my questioners acute and probing, on each of these occasions. I am deeply grateful.

In pulling these various lectures together into a single whole, I am very conscious that there are large swathes of Pauline thought still untouched. This book is not, in other words, in any sense a complete study of Paul. It does not attempt even to be particularly 'balanced'. What it does attempt to do, however, is to focus on some key areas of Paul's proclamation and its implications – including some not usually noticed – in an attempt to uncover 'what St Paul really said' at these vital points.

A few notes about some basic matters. There has been endless debate as to how far the Paul of the letters corresponds, or does not correspond, to the Paul we find in the Acts of the Apostles. I shall not engage in this debate here, though my analysis of what Paul was saying at key points in his letters may eventually turn out to have some bearing on the issue. Likewise, people still discuss at length whether Paul actually wrote all the letters attributed to him. Most of what I say in this book focuses on material in the undisputed letters, particularly Romans, the two Corinthian letters, Galatians and Philippians. In addition, I regard Colossians as certainly by Paul, and Ephesians as far more likely to be by him than by an imitator. But nothing in my present argument hinges on this one way or the other.

Apart from a few essential notes, I have not attempted to indicate the points at which I am building on, or taking issue with, colleagues within the discipline of Pauline studies. The detailed foundations of my argument can mostly be found in my own various published writings. These, and other works which may be helpful for further study, are listed in the bibliography. Scholarly colleagues will realize that the present work is not attempting to be a learned monograph; non-scholarly readers will perhaps forgive me my occasional forays into what seem to me, though they may not to them, necessary diversions and complexities.

After the work on this project was more or less complete, there appeared (in a review copy, sent to me at proof stage) a new book by the English journalist, novelist and biographer A.N. Wilson. He revives the old argument that Paul was the real founder of Christianity, misrepresenting Jesus and inventing a theology in which a 'Christ' figure, nothing really to do with the Jesus of history, becomes central. Since this theory turns up regularly in one guise or another, and since what I wanted to say in this book anyway forms the basis for the reply I think should be made, I have added at the end a chapter dealing with the whole issue, and with Wilson's book in particular. There are, of course, plenty of books that deal with this issue at great length, and I shall not attempt to duplicate their discussion.

The Bishop of Lichfield, the Right Reverend Keith Sutton, invited me to give the Selwyn Lectures in which some of these ideas had their first public airing. His support and friendship since my move to Lichfield have been a key element in my being able to continue with research and writing despite the demands of a busy Cathedral. His own example of Christian missionary work, and of bearing with joy the sufferings which come through it, have been to many of us a clear signpost to the reality by which Paul lived and of which he wrote. This book is dedicated to him as a small token of the love and gratitude which my family and I feel.

Tom Wright
Lichfield
Feast of the Conversion of St Paul, 1997

CHAPTER 1

Puzzling Over Paul

According to the Acts of the Apostles, Paul warned his converts in Asia that the path to the kingdom of God lay through many persecutions. Had there been any doubt on the matter, his own life would have been quite sufficient to show them what he meant. Threatened, attacked, misunderstood, shipwrecked, criticized, mocked, belittled, ridiculed, stoned, beaten, abused, insulted; that was his regular lot. Finally, perhaps the unkindest cut of all, he was canonized by the later church, thus enabling later readers to accuse him of posturing to gain power. (The church, however, has often made calling him 'Saint Paul' an excuse for failing either to understand him or to imitate him.)

I sometimes wonder what Paul would say about the treatment he has had in the twentieth century. *'Plus ça change, plus c'est la même chose'*, perhaps — always assuming that by now he would have added French to the impressive list of languages he already spoke. His fate in this century has been not unlike his fate in his own day. Nobody who wants to think about Christianity can ignore him; but they can, and do, abuse him, misunderstand him, impose their own categories on him, come to him with the wrong questions and wonder why he doesn't give a clear answer, and shamelessly borrow material from him to fit into other schemes of which he would not have approved. And when people proclaim most loudly that they are being Pauline, that the great apostle is their real guiding star, then we find often enough that they are elevating one aspect of his thinking above all the others, so much so that other aspects, for which he was equally concerned, are left to one side or even outrageously denied.

Often, as with the riot in Ephesus, one suspects that a lot of noise is made on both sides by people who aren't actually very sure what they are talking about. People who are afraid to tell God, or even Jesus, how angry they are with him or them, are often glad to be able to take such anger out on someone like Paul, about whom they cherish no such inhibitions.

Equally, people who clutch eagerly at a scheme of theology or religion might sometimes shrink from asserting that it represents the very mind of God himself, but by claiming Paul as an ally they have the comforting sense of possessing a friend at court. Paul, one may suspect, might be embarrassed by foe and friend alike, though I guess he has got used to it by now.

I would be naive if I imagined that I could escape these traps entirely myself. Thinking the thoughts of any great writer after him or her is a risky and tricky business. The best we can often do is an approximate guess. But the measure of success must always be to ask the question: does looking at Paul in a particular way illuminate passages that were previously puzzling? Does it enable his letters to gain a new coherence both with their particular situation and with one another? Does it give us a big overall picture of what Paul was about, without doing violence to the little details? Does it actually enhance the significance of those details? When we look at the treatment Paul has received in the twentieth century, we find again and again that the answer to all these questions is No. Gains in one area are balanced all too frequently by losses in another. My modest hope is that the same will not be true, or not to the same extent, in what I have to say.

Writing about Paul means joining a conversation that has already been in progress for a good while. Whole books have been written on the history of Pauline scholarship, and we can do no more than glance at one or two significant figures here. But we must at least glance: these are the people who have determined the way we approach Paul today, the questions we put to him and hence, in a measure, the answers we can expect.

Paul in the Twentieth Century

Schweitzer

The study of Paul this century[1] goes back, as does the study of Jesus, to the monumental work of Albert Schweitzer. Although his own study of Pauline theology[2] was delayed by many years through his concentration on medical missionary work, his earlier volume on Paul and his interpreters is still worth reading if we want to get a sense, albeit from one very definite and quite slanted point of view, of what was going on.[3] He analyzes the work of a good many writers by putting to them two quite simple questions, which have continued to dominate scholarship, and which will be important throughout this book. First, is Paul really a Jewish thinker or a Greek thinker? Second, what is the centre of Paul's theology? Is it (the two options Schweitzer considered as serious candidates) 'justification by faith', or 'being in Christ'? The two questions are interlocking: Schweitzer believed that 'being in Christ' was an essentially Jewish doctrine, while 'justification by faith' carried a strong implicit criticism of Judaism.

I believe Aim with fervently)

Schweitzer's own solution was never in doubt. He poured scorn on those who insisted on bringing pagan, Hellenistic categories to Paul as the best way of understanding him. Paul is Jewish through and through, he said, even though, precisely through his work as the Jewish apostle to the Gentiles, he prepared the way for the subsequent Hellenization of Christianity. Equally, Schweitzer argued that justification by faith, and the complex of issues that clusters around it, was not the heart and centre of Paul, but was rather a polemical thrust (emerging, after all, in only two letters and in a single passage in a third) relating to the very specific issue of the admission of uncircumcised Gentiles into the church. Rather, the centre of Paul was what Schweitzer called 'Christ-mysticism'. By this, he referred to the famous Pauline doctrine of 'being in Christ', and understood that doctrine against the background of apocalyptic Judaism. The God of Israel had acted in the world dramatically, apocalyptically, through Jesus the Messiah. The true people of God were now somehow bound up with this Messiah, this Christ. They were incorporated 'into' him.

Along with this analysis Schweitzer made plenty of significant decisions about how to read several key passages in Paul. Perhaps the best known is the effect of his view on how one reads the letter to the Romans, generally acknowledged as Paul's masterpiece. If you think that 'justification by faith' is the heart of Paul's theology, you may wish to stress Romans 1–4 as the real centre of the letter. If, with Schweitzer, you think that 'being in Christ' is the heart of Paul, you may wish to stress Romans 5–8 instead. (You might, of course, object that there is no reason why the specific argument of Romans, or indeed any other letter, should necessarily reflect the emphases of Paul's underlying theology; but Romans has regularly been forced to play this role whether it wants to or not, and Schweitzer is only one of many writers who have gone along with this game.)

A third question that accompanied Schweitzer's analysis of Paul was that of its practical consequence. What does Paul mean for today? For Schweitzer, I think, there were two meanings, positive and negative. First, if what mattered was 'being in Christ', rather than the logic-chopping debates about justification, then one was free to live out the life of Christ in new and different ways. This, I think, was part of what sustained Schweitzer himself in his unique and extraordinary life and work. Second, by the same token, one did not have to pay too much heed to what the official church was doing, since it was still stuck with Paul the dogmatic theologian. Schweitzer thus carved out his own path through the first half of this century, a lonely and learned giant amidst the hordes of noisy and shallow theological pygmies.

Schweitzer bequeathed to us, in a nutshell, the four questions that are always asked about Paul.

1. Where do we put Paul in the history of first-century religion?

2. How do we understand his theology, its starting point and centre?

3. How do we read the individual letters, getting out of them what Paul himself put into them (the scholars' word for this task is 'exegesis', as opposed to 'eisegesis', which means putting in a fresh meaning that Paul did not intend)?

4. And, what is the pay-off, the result, in terms of our own life and work today?

History, theology, exegesis and application: all writers on Paul implicitly or explicitly engage with these four questions. One of the reasons why Schweitzer is so important is that he saw them so clearly and, though his own solutions are variable in quality, he nevertheless provides a benchmark for subsequent study.

Bultmann

The next great twentieth-century expositor of Paul to be considered is Rudolf Bultmann.[4] In his *New Testament Theology*, he made Paul one of the twin pillars of his whole structure (the other being John). Paul provides, for Bultmann, a crucial analysis of the plight humans find themselves in, and of the means of escape. Bultmann uses the language both of Paul and of Luther, engaging with the great enemies of the human race (sin, the law, and death) and with the great solutions (grace, faith, righteousness, life). In this analysis, Bultmann drew heavily and explicitly on contemporary philosophy as well as historical research. In particular, he developed a form of the

German existentialism made famous by Martin Heidegger. The question remains as to whether Bultmann's theology, including his picture of Paul, is really a Christian version of existentialism or an existentialist version of Christianity.

Bultmann's answers to the four questions run more or less as follows. Paul belongs in his Hellenistic context; he was, after all, the apostle to the Gentiles, and he quickly abandoned the Jewish categories of his early thought and expressed his message in the categories, as well as the language, of the wider Greek world. He thus stood over against the Jewish world in which his fellow-countrymen, by embracing the law, were refusing the possibility of authentic existence offered in Christ, the end of the law. The heart and centre of Paul's theology, for Bultmann, was therefore his analysis of the human plight and of the decision ('faith') by which one might escape it. Paul, for Bultmann, retained the Jewish belief that the world was about to come to an end, but he made this a reason for abandoning the Jewish historical hopes and translating his message into the timeless categories of Greek thought.

When Bultmann read Romans, he (like Schweitzer but for very different reasons) found its centre in chapters 5–8, especially Romans 7 and 8. There, the plight of what Bultmann called 'man under the law' was graphically displayed. Practically, the thrust of Paul for today was to sustain Christians in their faith, as the world, including the world of Christian religion, crumbled all around them. We must remember that Bultmann, like Barth and others, achieved his theological maturity at the same time as the Nazi party was coming to power.

The price of Bultmann's brilliant synthesis is very high. Some parts of Paul just refused to fit into the scheme. These he therefore cheerfully demoted: he claimed that they were either 'glosses' (words or phrases added to Paul's text by later writers), or bits and pieces of Paul's Jewish background which Paul himself had not really thought through in the light of his mature theology. (I regard the claim to be able to think Paul's thoughts better than Paul could himself to be extremely dubious; but more about that later.)

Davies

Bultmann was enormously popular in the scholarly study of the New Testament for a good half of the present century. His work ensured that Schweitzer's plea to read Paul within his Jewish context fell all too often on deaf ears. The idea that Paul got his significant ideas, motifs and theology not from Judaism but from Hellenism remained intact in the work of a good many writers, sustained as they were by misreadings of Judaism itself, which we shall attend to presently. But just after World War II there came a great sea-change, heralded in the work of a young Welshman who was then to spend most of his life in the United States. W.D. Davies studied the Jewish rabbis in a way that, at that stage, few New Testament scholars had done. When he compared them with Paul he discovered that one after another of the features which Bultmann and others had attributed to Paul's Greek background could be found just as clearly in Judaism. Davies argued in his major work *Paul and Rabbinic Judaism* that Paul was, at bottom, a Jewish rabbi who believed that Jesus of Nazareth was the Jewish Messiah.[5]

Davies set the agenda to which much of post-war scholarship has been responding, either in elaboration or in reaction. He did not go down Schweitzer's road of making Paul an apocalyptic Jew, expecting the world to end at any moment; but, for all that, his work represents a turn back in Schweitzer's direction. He rejects outright the attempt to derive Paul's thought from Hellenism, and plants him firmly back into the soil of his native Judaism. Significantly, Davies, like Schweitzer, thereby held to one side Paul's critique of Judaism, both theologically and exegetically. Instead, Davies' Paul stresses that the Age to Come, long expected within Judaism, has arrived with Jesus. It has brought to birth a new people of God – with a new Torah (law), namely 'the law of Christ' (Galatians 6:2).

Davies' work signals a new attitude to Judaism on the part of post-war scholarship. Until then, Judaism had been regarded by most Pauline expositors as the great exemplar of the wrong sort of religion. It represented human self-effort, legalism, prejudice and pride. The reason Paul must have got his ideas from Hellenism, so it was thought, is that Jewish ones were irrevocably tainted. Even to use them was to compromise the faith. But with Davies the whole scene has changed, in line with the work of Karl Barth, with the so-called 'biblical theology' movement, and of course with the post-war reaction against the vile anti-Semitism which caused the Holocaust. Judaism was suddenly in vogue; Jewish ideas were regarded as good, and Hellenistic ones were labelled 'pagan' and therefore (implicitly) bad. The questions of history, theology, exegesis and application all therefore received a quite new emphasis as a result of Davies' work. Most scholars have not followed him all the way in his derivation of one Pauline point after another from rabbinic sources (many of them, as he knew, are after all to be dated some centuries later than Paul). But he at least demonstrated that one could not dislocate Paul from his Jewish setting without doing him great violence.

Käsemann

The fourth scholar we must look at briefly is Ernst Käsemann, Professor at Tübingen in the 1960s and 1970s. In many works, culminating in his magisterial commentary on Romans, he offered a new synthesis of Pauline theology.[6] Käsemann attempted to retain the strong points of both Schweitzer and Bultmann. On the one hand, he agreed with Schweitzer that Paul's true background was to be found in apocalyptic Judaism. On the other hand, he agreed with Bultmann and other Lutherans that the centre of Paul was to be found in his theology of justification, which struck at the heart of all human legalism and religious pride. This way of cutting the cake enabled Käsemann to do far more justice to the detail of Paul's writings than Bultmann. Käsemann was able to retrieve many parts of Paul that Bultmann's analysis had left scattered on the floor, and to stitch them back into something like their proper places. In particular, he argued that Paul was most of all concerned with the victory of the true God over the powers of evil and the whole rebellious world. God in Christ had won the great battle over evil, and was now at work to implement that victory through the preaching of the gospel. Human pride (not least *religious* pride) attempted to win the victory for itself rather than to accept the humbling victory of God. The justification of the ungodly (Romans 4:5) sets the record straight.

In Käsemann we get the first hint of a theme which, I shall suggest, is enormously important in our understanding of Paul: that, from within his Jewish context, Paul produced a *critique* of Judaism. Up to this point, in New Testament scholarship, it seemed to be assumed that if you were a Jewish thinker you would have little or no critique of Judaism – and that, conversely, if you clearly had a critique of Judaism you must have got it from somewhere else, from outside Judaism. Käsemann seems to recognize the point – which one might have thought would have been obvious from the Old Testament prophets, not to mention John the Baptist and Jesus – that *critique from within* was in fact a central feature of Judaism all along. His apocalyptically-minded Paul, therefore, announced to the world that the crucified Jesus was its rightful Lord, calling to account all human pride and rebellion, including Jewish pride and rebellion (seen especially in its attitude to its own law). For Käsemann, part of the application of this reading was a

17

more firmly grounded political theology than most of his predecessors had had. Käsemann had been part of the German Confessing Church under the Third Reich, and had even been imprisoned for his anti-Nazi activities. The sight of so much German petit-bourgeois religion meekly going along with Hitler, and using religious language to sustain such a stance, revolted him, and his life's work can be seen, in part, as a fierce attempt to ground his socio-political protest in serious and detailed exegesis of Paul.

If I had to choose the works of one Pauline exegete to take with me to a desert island, it would be Käsemann. The power, the drive, the exegetical honesty and thoroughness, the passion for truth and for freedom, are wonderful to read, and send me back to Paul again and again with fresh eyes. My very considerable disagreements with him should not mask this great admiration and gratitude. But the scholar who has affected current Pauline scholarship more than all the rest put together is Ed P. Sanders, a former colleague of mine in Oxford, now Professor at Duke University in Durham, North Carolina.[7]

Sanders

It is a measure of Sanders' achievement that Pauline scholars around the world now refer casually to 'the Sanders revolution'. Even those who are hostile to his theories cannot deny that there has indeed been a great turn-around in scholarship, so much so that many books written before Sanders, or from a pre-Sanders standpoint, now look extremely dated and actually feel very boring — something no writer on Paul ought to be! Though I myself disagree strongly with Sanders on some points, and want to go a good deal further than him on some others, there is no denying that he has towered over the last quarter of the century much as Schweitzer and Bultmann did over the first half.

Sanders' major work on Paul is entitled *Paul and Palestinian Judaism*. The echo of Davies was deliberate; Davies was one of Sanders' teachers, and Sanders saw himself as continuing his emphasis, though in various new ways. Instead of reading Paul simply against his rabbinic background, he sketched out a much broader canvas of Palestinian Judaism in Paul's day, looking at the Dead Sea Scrolls (which of course were not available when Davies first wrote), the apocrypha and pseudepigrapha, the wisdom literature, and so on. His major point, to which all else is subservient, can be quite simply stated. Judaism in Paul's day was not, as has regularly been supposed, a religion of legalistic works-righteousness. If we imagine that it was, and that Paul was attacking it as if it was, we will do great violence to it and to him. Most Protestant exegetes had read Paul and Judaism as if Judaism was a form of the old heresy Pelagianism, according to which humans must pull themselves up by their moral bootstraps and thereby earn justification, righteousness, and salvation. No, said Sanders. Keeping the law within Judaism always functioned within a covenantal scheme.[8] God took the initiative, when he made a covenant with Judaism; God's grace thus precedes everything that people (specifically, Jews) do in response. The Jew keeps the law out of gratitude, as the proper response to grace – not, in other words, in order to *get* into the covenant people, but to *stay* in. Being 'in' in the first place was God's gift. This scheme Sanders famously labelled as 'covenantal nomism' (from the Greek *nomos*, law). Keeping the Jewish law was the human response to God's covenantal initiative.

Sanders thus, at a stroke, cut the ground from under the majority reading of Paul, especially in mainline Protestantism. Judaism, he insisted, was and is a perfectly valid and proper form of religion. Paul's only real critique of Judaism, according to Sanders, was that it was 'not Christianity'. Paul, having found salvation in Christianity, was forced to conclude that Judaism was not enough. The centre of Paul's thought (here Sanders sides very firmly with Schweitzer) was not justification, nor his critique of Israel; the centre was what Sanders calls 'participation', Sanders' word for the complex of Pauline thought which focuses on 'being in Christ'.

One of the ironies in Sanders' position is that he has never really carried through his reform into a thorough rethinking of Paul's own thought. He contents himself with a somewhat unsystematic treatment of different Pauline themes. Nor has he offered very much verse-by-verse exegesis, the real test of how a particular scheme works out in practice. But his practical agenda is very clear: Christians should regard Jews with a good deal more respect than in the past, and in particular should not saddle them with a form of religion of which they are innocent. Pauline Christians and the successors of first-century Palestinian Judaism should not anathematize each other as they have often been wont to do.

The aftermath of the 'Sanders revolution' has been revealing. Some have leapt on to the bandwagon with indecent haste – eager, perhaps, to embrace Sanders' relativistic conclusions, and careless of his exegetical foundations, his historical reconstruction, or (such as they are) his theological architectonics. Others, especially within conservative circles, have reacted with hostility, doing their best to rehabilitate the old view of Judaism as a form of proto-Pelagianism, and the old reading of Paul as the preacher of justification by faith in the sense of a way of salvation that renounces human self-effort ('works of the law'). In Germany, many Pauline scholars regard Sanders simply as a dangerous menace who doesn't know what he's talking about. He nevertheless dominates the landscape, and, until a major refutation of his central thesis is produced, honesty compels one to do business with him. I do not myself believe such a refutation can or will be offered; serious modifications are required, but I regard his basic point as established.

Today's Questions

The current situation in Pauline studies is pleasantly confused. I suspect, actually, that it always has been; it is only with hindsight that one can observe major trends and significant shifts of opinion. Now, as probably in most periods, there are large numbers of people doing bewilderingly different things with Paul. Each of the four major questions is being studied. A few words are in order on each of them.

History

Almost all scholars now regard Paul as a very Jewish thinker, though the question of which bits of Judaism he stands closest to, and how much of his Judaism was rethought in the light of the gospel, is much disputed. (We now know, of course, a great deal more about first-century Judaism than we did even a generation ago.) Other issues of how to place Paul historically have come up. Sociology and the study of ancient writing-techniques ('rhetoric') attempt to locate him within different aspects of the culture of his day. There are still one or two writers who try to make Paul a thoroughgoing Hellenist (unlike the attempts earlier this century, these are usually done in order to blacken Paul's reputation) but they do not command much assent.

Theology

There is no agreement on the centre of Paul's theology. Most German writers on Paul, and some within conservative North American circles, still insist on the cross and justification as the centre of Paul's thinking; but this is widely controverted, and indeed the whole question of *how* we can tell what the centre of anyone's thought might be, or indeed whether that question even makes sense, has worried many mainstream scholars in the last decade. The currently fashionable category of 'story' or 'narrative' has been employed as a way into his theology, though there is currently no agreement on how to use the category, or what might happen if we did. The dislocation of biblical studies from theology, particularly in many North American institutions (where the majority of contemporary biblical studies takes place) has meant that Paul is often studied by people who are not trained either philosophically or theologically, and who indeed resent the idea that such training should be necessary. Many New Testament scholars use detailed exegesis as a way of escaping from heavy-handed and stultifying conservatism; any attempt to articulate an overarching Pauline theology looks to them like an attempt to reconstruct the sort of system from which they themselves are glad to be free. As in some other scholarly circles, using the study of history to exorcise one's own past is an attractive, though one suspects ineffective, form of therapy.

Exegesis

The study of Paul's letters, in detail, has proceeded apace, with ever more primary sources being consulted, both in Jewish and pagan writers, to provide parallels to Paul's usage and ideas. Likewise, there has been such a flood of secondary literature, of very varying quality, that the commentator who wants to be thorough confronts a huge task of wading through the journals and attempting to do justice to what may be found there. Recent commentaries have thus tended to be repositories of detailed learning rather than major theological statements. This may be no bad thing, provided we realize that the ground is thereby prepared for further theological readings in the future, building (we may hope) on what is best in the mass of detailed study now so readily, but so tantalizingly, available.

Application

The question of how we use Paul for today remains as firmly on the table as ever. Some still play the reductionist game of imagining that if we put Paul in his historical context we can leave him there; that is itself a proposal about current interpretation, namely the proposal that we should leave Paul out of the account in constructing our own worldview and theology. Some still use him to legitimate an old-style 'preaching of the gospel' in which the basic problem is human sin and pride and the basic answer is the cross of Christ. Others, without wishing to deny this as part of the Pauline message, are struggling to do justice to the wider categories and the larger questions that seem to be a non-negotiable part of Paul's whole teaching. This, indeed, is the category into which I would put myself, as the present work will make clear. There are all sorts of possibilities here for addressing the specific questions of the 1990s, and indeed the 2000s, and in doing so, discovering the relevance of parts of Paul formerly relegated to comparative obscurity. When, for instance, we confront the serious neo-paganism of the Western world, with its rampant materialism on the one hand and its 'new age' philosophies on the other, it is no bad time to remind ourselves (as we shall in a subsequent chapter) that Paul's basic mission was to the pagans of his world, not to the Jews, and that he might just have something to say to contemporary paganism as well. But more of this anon.

As we sharpen our scholarly lenses in order to bring Paul himself into focus, we begin to glimpse in the background a larger question of which he is a vital part. What was the role of Paul in the foundation of Christianity? Was Paul the true interpreter of Jesus? Or was he a maverick innovator who invented a new religion, nothing to do with what Jesus had intended, in which the figure of 'Jesus' happened to play a central role?

This is the argument of one or two contemporary writers on Paul, particularly some from within a Jewish frame of reference. Hyam Maccoby, a well-known Jewish scholar and apologist, has argued in a number of books that Jesus, who (he says) has been well and truly obscured by the Christian 'gospels', was in fact a Pharisee, a good and loyal Jew who would not have dreamed of breaking with Judaism on any central point, let alone inventing a new religion. Paul, however, says Maccoby, was never a Pharisee (despite Paul's own explicit claim); he was always on the margins of Judaism, a thoroughly Hellenized thinker who then reinterpreted Jesus within a Greek, perhaps even a Gnostic, frame of thought. He succeeded only in producing a 'Jesus' who was the product of his own peculiar religio/philosophical imagination, a figure who bore no relation to Jesus himself and who belonged in the world of Greek religion, a cult-god. Paul, according to Maccoby, thus paved the way for subsequent Western anti-Semitism.

A.N. Wilson, a writer and journalist who publicly renounced Christianity some years ago, and then wrote a book about Jesus designed, in part, to

22

justify this personal move, has now produced a book on Paul which falls into much the same category. Unaware, it seems, of the warnings of Schweitzer against those who bring Hellenistic concepts to Paul to explain him when obvious Jewish ones lie much closer to hand, he somewhat patronizingly describes Paul as a very great thinker — but who missed the main point of what Jesus was all about. Paul is the real 'founder of Christianity', using Hellenistic categories to interpret what, in his somewhat muddled but enthusiastic way, he supposed the meaning of Jesus might be. In these two instances, and in many similar ones, we shall see as the present book progresses that such theories are wandering in the foggy foothills of the discussion, while far above them, clear and striking, stand the peaks and glaciers, the cliffs and ledges, which constitute the real high ground of Pauline thought.

Paul in the twentieth century, then, has been used and abused much as in the first. Can we, as the century draws towards its close, listen a bit more closely to him? Can we somehow repent of the ways we have mishandled him and respect his own way of doing things a bit more? This book is an attempt to do just that: to stand back from the ways we have read Paul and to explore a bit more how Paul himself suggests we read him. It is an attempt to study Paul in his own terms. It is trying to come to grips with what he really said.

Notes

1. On all of what follows, there is a fuller account in Stephen Neill and N.T. Wright, *The Interpretation of the New Testament, 1861–1986,* 1988, pages 403–30.

2. Albert Schweitzer, *The Mysticism of Paul the Apostle,* 1968 [1930].

3. Albert Schweitzer, *Paul and his Interpreters: A Critical History,* 1912.

4. Rudolf Bultmann, *Theology of the New Testament,* 1951–55.

5. W.D. Davies, *Paul and Rabbinic Judaism,* 1980 (3rd edition; 1st edition 1948).

6. Ernst Käsemann, *Perspectives on Paul,* 1969, *New Testament Questions of Today,* 1971, *Commentary on Romans,* 1980.

7. E.P. Sanders, *Paul and Palestinian Judaism: A Comparison of Patterns of Religion,* 1977; *Paul, the Law, and the Jewish People,* 1983; *Paul,* 1991.

8. See below, page 29 and following, for a fuller explanation of covenant.

CHAPTER 2

Saul the Persecutor, Paul the Convert

The Agendas of Saul of Tarsus

In Romans 10:2 Paul writes of his fellow Jews, in a phrase which undoubtedly carries autobiographical overtones: 'I bear them witness that they have a zeal for God, but it is not according to knowledge.' This becomes explicitly autobiographical in Philippians 3:6, where Paul describes himself as having been 'in terms of zeal, a persecutor of the church'. In Galatians 1:13-14 this becomes not only explicit but detailed:

> You have heard of my former life in Judaism, how thoroughly I ravaged the church of God and tried to destroy it; and I advanced in Judaism beyond many of my own age among my kinsmen, being exceedingly zealous for the traditions of my fathers.[1]

'Zeal', as we shall see, is a key term to characterize the sort of Jew, and the sort of Jewish agenda, that the young Saul of Tarsus had pursued.[2] But what were these agendas? And what happened to Saul, to turn him from a persecutor into a preacher?

The historical starting-point for investigating Saul of Tarsus must, of course, be the autobiographical remarks I quoted above, coupled with others such as 1 Corinthians 15:9. Despite a few writers such as Hyam Maccoby, whom I mentioned in the first chapter, it is completely implausible to suggest that Paul invented a fictitious autobiography. It is more likely by far that everybody in the early church knew of his persecuting activity, and that it was a background he could not avoid, but was bound to carry with shame wherever he went. If we are to understand the nature of Paul's conversion, and the shape of his thought after it as well as before, we must get this background straight.

Which type of Pharisee?

Saul's persecution of the church, and the word 'zeal' with which he describes it, puts him firmly on the map of a certain type of first-century Judaism. It gives us access to quite a wide database with which to plot the sort of agendas he must have been following, agendas which make sense of his activity in persecuting the church even beyond the borders of the Holy Land itself. It reveals Saul of Tarsus not just as a Jew, but as a Pharisee; not just as a Pharisee, but as a Shammaite Pharisee; not just, perhaps, as a Shammaite Pharisee, but as one of the strictest of the strict.

Who were the Shammaites? A division had taken place within Pharisaism in the generation before Saul of Tarsus. During the reign of Herod the Great (36–4BC) there arose two schools of thought within the already powerful movement, following the two great teachers of the Herodian period, Hillel and Shammai. We know them through dozens of discussions in the Mishnah (the codification of Jewish law, drawn together around AD200), where almost always Hillel is the 'lenient' one, and Shammai is the 'strict' one. Their followers, likewise, argue issue after issue in terms of lenient and strict practices.

By the time the Mishnah was written, around the end of the second century AD, the Hillelite position had already won the day, as indeed it does in most of the Mishnah itself. However, between the time of Hillel and Shammai in the later first century BC, and the time of the great Rabbi Akiba in the early years of the second century AD, there was still a good deal of controversy between these two branches of the Pharisees. Saul would have grown up in a world of fierce debate and party loyalty. Not only was he a Jew in a world run by pagan *goyim*, Gentiles, not only was he a Pharisee in a world where (from the Pharisees' point of view) many Jews were seriously compromised with aspects of paganism, he was a Shammaite, a hard-line Pharisee – what we today would call a militant right-winger.

But what precisely were Hillel and Shammai lenient and strict *about*? The Mishnah and the other later rabbinic writings give us the impression that they are lenient or strict about the personal observance of the commands of Torah. Things were not, however, quite so simple in Paul's world. The key issue at stake between 'lenient' and 'strict' interpretations of the law was not just a matter of religion. Nor was it just about private or personal piety. The key issue was as much 'political' as it was 'theological'. It was about aims and agendas for Israel: for the people, the land, and the Temple.

The question, as for many Jews in most of Jewish history, was: what line do we adopt *vis-à-vis* the present political situation? The Hillelites, broadly speaking, pursued a policy of 'live and let live'. Let the Herods and the Pilates, and indeed the Caiaphases, rule the world – let them even rule Israel, politically – just as long as we Jews are allowed to study and practise Torah (the Jewish law) in peace. The Shammaites believed that this wasn't good enough. Torah itself, they thought, demanded that Israel be free from the Gentile yoke, free to serve God in peace, calling no-one master except YHWH, the one true God, himself.

This is what it means to be 'zealous for God' or 'zealous for the traditions of the fathers' in first-century Judaism. We use the word 'zeal' to indicate warmth of heart and spirit, eagerness for a cause. That is a not inaccurate summary of one part of its first-century meaning, too. But whereas for the modern Christian 'zeal' is something you do on your knees, or in evangelism, or in works of charity, for the first-century Jew 'zeal' was something you did with a knife. Those first-century Jews who longed for revolution against Rome looked back to Phinehas and Elijah in the Old Testament, and to the Maccabean heroes two centuries before Paul, as their models. They saw themselves as being 'zealous for YHWH', 'zealous for Torah', and as having the right, and the duty, to put that zeal into operation with the use of violence. 'Zeal' thus comes close to holy war: a war to be fought (initially, at any rate) guerrilla-style, by individuals committed to the cause.

We should not imagine that such revolutionary activities were confined to a few hotheads, or to one short period (such as that leading up to the war of AD66–70). There is ample evidence of revolutionary activity throughout the first century before Jesus and the first century after him. And the people involved in it included, surprising though this may be to some, the majority of the Pharisees, namely, the Shammaites. The Jewish revolutionaries in this period were thus not simply political revolutionaries, unconcerned with religious or theological issues. As with some contemporary Muslim extremists, their reading of their sacred texts, fuelled by prayer and fasting, generated their revolutionary zeal in the first place and sustained it once it was up and running. Archaeology has shown that the revolutionary 'Sicarii', the 'dagger-men', who died in the last stand on Masada, were deeply pious Jews.

So far as our evidence allows us to be sure, the Shammaites were in the ascendancy in the time between Herod the Great and the Jewish-Roman war of AD66–70. There were notable Hillelites during this period, among whom we may note Gamaliel, who is described briefly in Acts 5:34-39. He argues precisely for the live-and-let-live position: if this new movement (Christianity) is not from God, it will fall by its own weight; but if it is from God, you had better not oppose it. The Gamaliels of the time, however, were outnumbered by those bent on revolutionary zeal. This zeal is well described by Josephus in a number of passages, and provides a picture of the Shammaite Pharisees, zealous for God, zealous for Torah, ready to go anywhere and do anything, up to and including violence, that would achieve the longed-for liberty, the long-awaited kingdom of God. Granted that there may not have been a single movement called 'the Zealots' throughout the first century, it is still clear that what many Jews called 'zeal for Torah' was a widespread phenomenon, particularly and precisely among the hard-line Shammaites. In short, as various writers (including myself) have argued elsewhere, the extreme right wing of the Shammaites merged into the general viewpoint which we might think of as 'zeal' – zeal for a holy revolution in which the pagans would be defeated once and for all, and in which as well, renegade Jews would either be brought into line or be destroyed along with the pagans.

A word of contemporary relevance at this point, with due caution about the danger of anachronism. If you want to see roughly what Shammaite Pharisaism was all about, look at the philosophy which inspired Yigal Amir to shoot Yitzhak Rabin in Tel Aviv on 4 November 1995. Amir was described as a 'law student'. This didn't mean he was training to be a solicitor or barrister in the Western sense, but that he was a student of Torah. And, as came through very clearly in all the news reports, he believed, with the backing of some senior rabbis in Israel and in America, that Rabin was a traitor, that he had sold out to the pagans, because he was prepared for the sake of peace to trade one of the greatest ancestral symbols, namely land.

When I saw Amir's face on the front page of the London *Times*, and read the report, I realized with a shock that I was looking at a twentieth-century version of Saul of Tarsus. Amir's position was completely logical. He was not mad. He knew he was right. The whole land, including the West Bank (called by the Jewish settlers 'Judea and Samaria') belongs to Israel, because the Torah says so. Those who compromise, not least those who compromise in order to flirt with the enemy, are *apikorsim*, traitors. The widespread horror among the vast majority of Jews, in Israel and around the world, at Amir's action mirrors the ancient Jewish attitude of Gamaliel and others. But he had grasped what 'zeal for Torah' means. This 'zeal' is not pietistic or apolitical. It is certainly not non-violent. It is all about acting as God's agent, to rid Israel of corruption, and so to further the agenda of bringing the kingdom, of freeing Israel from the pagan yoke. I would not want to make the mistake of suggesting that Amir's actions and Saul's were exactly alike. But Amir is a far better model for understanding the young man from Tarsus than a good many that have been cherished over the years. He may serve to remind us, at least, that there was more to zeal than fervent prayer and self-righteous religiosity.

After the destruction of the Temple in AD70, the Hillelites and Shammaites seem to have been more evenly matched, with Johanan ben Zakkai leading the Hillelites and Eleazar ben Hyrcanus a strong voice within the Shammaites. The key issue then became: do we or don't we seek to recapture Jerusalem, to rebuild the Temple, to throw off the Roman yoke? The Hillelites, seen in our evidence only through a haze of later Hillelite (and non- or anti-revolutionary) hagiography, urged that only Torah mattered. The loss of the Temple was not after all so tragic, since one could still study and practise Torah and thereby enjoy the presence of God just as though one were in the Temple. The Shammaites insisted that further violent revolution was still necessary: only the full liberation of Israel, and the rebuilding of the Temple, would do. At the end of this period, Akiba, hailed subsequently even by the Hillelites as one of the greatest rabbis of all time, threw in his lot with the revolution of Simeon ben Kosiba, declaring that he was the Messiah, 'the son of the star', come to fight the holy war against the pagans.

The beliefs and hopes of Saul

Where does Saul of Tarsus belong on this map of first-century Pharisaic belief and activity? In one of the speeches in Acts (22:3) he claims that Gamaliel had been one of his teachers. This, coupled with other evidence from the epistles, has led some scholars to suppose that he was a Hillelite before his conversion. This simply cannot be the case – unless all the evidence of his persecuting activity is a later fabrication, which seems highly unlikely. The Gamaliel of Acts 5 would not have approved of the stoning of Stephen. He would never have dreamed of riding off to Damascus to haul

Christians into prison and to death. Saul may have learned a lot from Gamaliel, but he did not share his particular position. If later, as a Christian, he argues for positions (on divorce, for instance) which are more like those of the Hillelites, that must be seen as part of the effect of his conversion, not as reflecting the agendas he had embraced in his pre-Christian state.

We may, then, sketch a picture of the agendas of a Shammaite Pharisee in the days of Saul of Tarsus, with some confidence that we are describing Saul himself. First, he believed passionately that the great prophetic promises had not yet been fulfilled. He lived on passages such as Daniel 2, 7 and 9, believing that they promised the coming kingdom of God very soon. These passages, in their historical context (whether fictive or otherwise), ostensibly spoke of the end of the Babylonian exile. However, as we know from other re-readings of Daniel in the first century, such as that of the apocryphal book known as 4 Ezra, there was no problem in mentally deleting 'Babylon' and substituting 'Rome'.

It was clear that the predictions of all the great prophets had yet to be fulfilled. The story was still incomplete. Israel had not been restored. Zechariah's ten men had not taken hold of the skirt of a Jew saying 'we will go with you, for we have heard that God is with you' (Zechariah 8:23); nor had YHWH taken his stand on Mount Zion to defeat all the nations that oppose Jerusalem (Zechariah 14:1-5). Ezekiel's new Temple had not been built, with rivers of healing water flowing out to make even the Dead Sea fresh (Ezekiel 47). And, towering over them all, Isaiah's vision of comfort, forgiveness, peace and prosperity had never been remotely near fulfilment (Isaiah 40–55). The Pharisees, and a good many Jews not aligned with any particular party, were still waiting for the great events to happen 'according to the scriptures'. They were still in exile. As the Qumran texts witness so poignantly, people were on tiptoe to believe that the real return from exile was about to happen – was, maybe, already beginning to happen, perhaps in secret.

The theology which sustained the revolutionaries thus included a reading of Israel's scriptures which told them in no uncertain terms where they were living in God's plan and what they should do to further it. Saul, like a great many Jews of his day, read the Jewish Bible not least as a story in search of an ending; and he conceived of his own task as being to bring that ending about. The story ran like this. Israel had been called to be the covenant people of the creator God, to be the light that would lighten the dark world, the people through whom God would undo the sin of Adam and its effects. But Israel had become sinful, and as a result had gone into exile, away from her own land. Although she had returned geographically from her exile, the real exilic condition was not yet finished. The promises had not yet been fulfilled. The Temple had not yet been rebuilt. The Messiah had not yet come. The pagans had not yet been reduced to submission, nor had they begun to make pilgrimages to Zion to learn Torah. Israel was still deeply compromised and sinful.

Into this situation, the scriptures spoke clearly and powerfully of the time that would surely come when all these things would be put right. This was not simply a matter of a few scattered prophecies, taken at random, predicting from a great distance odd bits and pieces of things that would come to pass one day. Scripture told the story; Israel lived in the story; the story was moving towards its appointed conclusion. One day soon YHWH would be king of all the earth; evil would be decisively defeated; Israel, or at least the true Jews within Israel, would be vindicated as the true people of the one true God. This reading of scripture, which fuelled the zeal of the Shammaite, could be summarized theologically in the following way. There are three cardinal points of Jewish theology in this period: monotheism, election and eschatology. There is one God, the one true God of all the world; Israel is the people of this one true God; and there is one future for all the world, a future not very far away now, in which the true God will reveal himself, defeat evil, and rescue his people. Believing all this, Saul of Tarsus was acting as best he knew 'according to the scriptures', understanding them not as a collection of proof-texts but as a story in search of an ending, an ending that he would himself help to bring about.

The Shammaites, and the revolutionaries in general, were eager to bring these prophecies to fulfilment by their zeal for Torah. They would not sit around and wait; they would take matters into their own hands. This was also, explicitly, a zeal for God, as Paul refers to it in Romans 10:2. The one true God, YHWH, was dishonoured by the present state of things; his glory demanded that the pagans, idol-worshippers as they were, would receive what they deserved. YHWH would become king of all the world. For this to happen, Israel needed to keep Torah. Observing Torah would hasten the time of fulfilment. If God were to act climactically now, within history, while Israel was still not keeping Torah properly, she would be condemned along with the Gentiles. But for Israel to keep Torah she would need to be reminded, indeed urged, to this task; again, with due awareness of the problem of anachronism, we may compare the way in which today's ultra-orthodox Jews insist upon the keeping of the sabbath, and enforce it, so far as they are able, with holy violence such as the stoning of cars driven through their quarter of the city. This is zeal in practice: zeal for God, zeal for Torah, zeal that will bring in the kingdom.

We must emphasize one thing at this point. The picture I have drawn is very different from the picture of the pre-Christian Saul that I grew up with. I was taught, and assumed for many years, that Saul of Tarsus believed what many of my contemporaries believed: that the point of life was to go to heaven when you die, and that the way to go to heaven after death was to adhere strictly to an overarching moral code. Saul, I used to believe, was a proto-Pelagian, who thought he could pull himself up by his moral bootstraps. What mattered for him was understanding, believing and operating a system of salvation that could be described as 'moralism' or 'legalism': a timeless system into which one plugged oneself in order to receive the promised benefits, especially 'salvation' and 'eternal life', understood as the post-mortem bliss of heaven.

I now believe that this is both radically anachronistic (this view was not invented in Saul's day) and culturally out of line (it is not the Jewish way of thinking). To this extent, I am convinced, Ed Sanders is right: we have misjudged early Judaism, especially Pharisaism, if we have thought of it as an early version of Pelagianism. Sanders does not, however, escape anachronism himself. He still analyzes Judaism in terms of 'religion', without integrating the political dimension in the way I have suggested. To this extent, he is following the Mishnah, trying to understand first-century Judaism in an essentially non-political religious sense. Like the Mishnah, he is tacitly embracing the Hillelite position.

But Saul of Tarsus was not interested in a timeless system of salvation, whether of works-righteousness or anything else. Nor was he interested simply in understanding and operating a system of religion, a system of 'getting in' and/or 'staying in' (Sanders' categories). He wanted God to redeem Israel. Moreover, he drew freely on texts from the Hebrew Bible which promised that Israel's God would do exactly that. He stood alongside other Jews of various persuasions, some of whose works have come down to us, who, out of great historical, cultural and political tribulation longed for their God to act within history on their behalf. This point is clearly of enormous importance, but I cannot do more than repeat it in case there is any doubt: Jews like Saul of Tarsus were not interested in an abstract, timeless, ahistorical system of salvation. They were not even primarily interested in, as we say today, 'going to heaven when they died'. (They believed in the resurrection, in which God would raise them all to share in the life of the promised renewed Israel and renewed world; but that is very different from the normal Western vision of 'heaven'.) They were interested in the salvation which, they believed, the one true God had promised to his people Israel.

One feature of this hope needs special attention at this point. The purpose of the covenant, in the Hebrew Bible and in some subsequent writings, was never simply that the creator wanted to have Israel as a special people, irrespective of the fate of the rest of the world. The purpose of the covenant was that, through this means, the creator would address and save his entire world. The call of Abraham was designed to undo the sin of Adam. But, as the exile made clear, Israel needed redeeming; the messenger needed a message of salvation. The people with the solution had become part of the problem. And, as I said before, most first-century Jews did not believe the exile had ended. The Temple had not been rebuilt properly; the Messiah had not yet arrived; the general resurrection had not occurred; the Torah was not being observed perfectly; the Gentiles were not flocking in to hear the word of the Lord on Mount Zion. Until these things had happened, God's purposes and promises had not come to pass.

This sets us up to understand two technical terms which we shall find it hard to do without. First, what would 'justification' mean in this context? 'Justification' is a law-court term, and in its Jewish context it refers to the greatest lawsuit of all: that which will take place on the great day when the true God judges all the nations, more particularly the nations that have been oppressing Israel. God will, at last, find in favour of his people: he will judge the pagan nations and rescue his true people. 'Justification' thus describes the coming great act of redemption and salvation, *seen from the point of view* of the covenant (Israel is God's people) on the one hand and the law court on the other (God's final judgment will be like a great law-court scene, with Israel winning the case). Learning to 'see' an event in terms of two great themes like these is part of learning how first-century Jews understood the world.

The law-court metaphor was vital to the underlying meaning of the covenant. The covenant was there in the first place to deal with the sin of the world, and (to the Hebrew mind) you dealt with sin through the law court, condemning the sinner and 'justifying', i.e. acquitting or vindicating, the righteous. It was therefore utterly appropriate that this great event, the final sorting-out of all things, should be described in terms drawn from the law court. God himself was the judge; evildoers (i.e. the Gentiles, and renegade

Jews) would finally be judged and punished; God's faithful people (i.e. Israel, or at least the true Israelites) would be vindicated. Their redemption, which would take the physical and concrete form of political liberation, the restoration of the Temple, and ultimately of resurrection itself, would be *seen as* the great law-court showdown, the great victory before the great judge. The book of Daniel, especially chapter 7, provides several instances of this scenario. Not surprisingly, Daniel was a great favourite with the revolutionaries.

The second major technical term that we cannot easily escape is 'eschatology'. Look this word up in the dictionary, and you will probably find something like 'the doctrine of death, judgment, heaven and hell'. When scholars use the word in relation to first-century Judaism and Christianity, though, they mean something rather different. They use it to denote the Jewish and Christian belief that Israel's history, and thereby world history, was moving towards a great climactic moment in which everything would be sorted out once and for all. (A red herring has been drawn across the trail at this point by a routine failure to understand that when Jews and early Christians used 'end-of-the-world' *language* to describe this phenomenon they didn't mean it literally. They did not suppose that the world and history were actually going to come to an end. They used 'end-of-the-world' language to invest major and cataclysmic events *within* history with their (as we might say) 'earth-shattering' significance.) 'Eschatology' thus refers to the belief that history was going to reach, or perhaps that it had just reached, its great climax, its great turning-point. Both the language they used to say this, and the belief itself, are also sometimes referred to as 'apocalyptic', though this has become so slippery a technical term that some scholars have given up using it altogether.

Put these two (justification and eschatology) together, and what happens? 'Justification', the great moment of salvation seen in terms of the fulfilment of the covenant and in terms of the last great law-court scene, would thus also be *eschatological*: it would be the final fulfilment of Israel's long-cherished hope. Putting it another way, the Jewish eschatological hope was hope for justification, for God to vindicate his people at last.

This event, this final justification, could be *anticipated* under certain circumstances. Particular Jews, by keeping the Torah with particular zeal, could reckon themselves to be already the 'true Israel'. I shall say more about this in chapter 7.

What, then, was the agenda of Saul of Tarsus? We may draw it together in three points. First, he was zealous for Israel's God and for the Torah. This was a matter of personal piety, no doubt, and of fervent prayer and study. His zeal for Torah was not, however, a Pelagian religion of self-help moralism. It was zeal to see God honoured which necessitated stamping out, by whatever means were necessary, all forms of disloyalty to the Torah among Jews, and throwing off, again by whatever means might be necessary, the pagan yoke which polluted Israel's land and prevented her from attaining the freedom that was her covenantal birthright. Second, Saul intended that he and others should keep Torah so wholeheartedly in the present that they would be marked out already as those who would be vindicated on the great coming day when YHWH finally acted to save and redeem his people. Third, he intended to hasten this day by forcing other Jews to keep the Torah in his way, using violence as and when necessary. For him, these three things went closely together. They provided a private and personal, as well as a political and public, set of aims and goals. It was in pursuit of these goals that he obtained authority from the chief priests – we may note that, as a Pharisee, he didn't have any such right himself – to go off to Damascus to seize Christians, men and women alike, and to drag them off to prison. They were renegade Jews, leading Israel astray from true loyalty to the one true God. That is how he came to be travelling, on a day that any historian would regard as of major significance for subsequent world history, on the road to Damascus.

Saul's Conversion and its Immediate Significance

Damascus road: the event and its significance

Paul was adamant, in referring to his conversion experience, that he really had seen Jesus. He was aware, as appears from 1 Corinthians 15, that the other apostles had seen Jesus alive after his death in what might be termed the 'ordinary' sequence of resurrection appearances, and that he had had the same sighting of Jesus but at a time when the others had ceased to see Jesus. Borrowing Luke's language, Paul saw the risen Jesus even after the ascension. The language he uses is not the language of mystical vision, of spiritual or religious experiences without any definite objective referent. Paul did not think he went on seeing Jesus in this way in his subsequent continuing Christian experience, though he remained intensely conscious of his presence, love and sustaining power. He uses the language of actual seeing.

This fact must be stressed because Paul's awareness of Jesus as having been bodily raised from the dead is of paramount importance in understanding the significance of what happened to him on the road to Damascus. It will not do, historically speaking, to spiritualize or psychologize the event, as though (for instance) Saul had been labouring with a troubled conscience for years and suddenly had a great religious experience which enabled him to throw off the burden and enjoy a new level or dimension of spiritual existence. Nor will it do simply to say, as so many have done, (a) that Saul of Tarsus had formerly regarded the crucified Jesus as cursed by the Jewish law; (b) that he then realized that God had reversed the law's curse; so (c) he realized that the law was now shown up as bankrupt and out of date, and (d) he could begin to announce to the world that there was a way of being the people of God in which the law played no role. Even if any of this carries a grain of truth, it is not central to what was going on.

The significance of Jesus' resurrection, for Saul of Tarsus as he lay blinded and perhaps bruised on the road to Damascus, was this. *The one true God had done for Jesus of Nazareth, in the middle of time, what Saul had thought he was going to do for Israel at the end of time.* Saul had imagined that YHWH would vindicate *Israel* after her suffering at the hand of the pagans. Instead, he had vindicated *Jesus* after his suffering at the hand of the pagans. Saul had imagined that the great reversal, the great apocalyptic event, would take place all at once, inaugurating the kingdom of God with a flourish of trumpets, setting all wrongs to right, defeating evil once and for all, and ushering in the age to come. Instead, the great reversal, the great resurrection, had happened to one man, all by himself. What could this possibly mean?

Quite simply, it meant this: Jesus of Nazareth, whose followers had regarded him as the Messiah, the one who would bear the destiny of Israel, had seemed to Saul rather to be an anti-Messiah, someone who had failed to defeat the pagans, and had succeeded only in generating a group of people who were sitting loose to the Torah and critical of the Temple, two of the great symbols of Jewish identity. But the resurrection demonstrated that Jesus' followers were right. In his greatest letter, Paul put it like this: Jesus the Messiah was descended from the seed of David according to the flesh, and *marked out as the Son of God* (i.e. Messiah) *by the Spirit of holiness through the resurrection of the dead* (Romans 1:4). The resurrection demarcated Jesus as the true Messiah, the true bearer of Israel's God-sent destiny.

But if Jesus really was the Messiah, and if his death and resurrection really were the decisive heaven-sent defeat of sin and vindication of the people of YHWH, then this means that the Age to Come had already begun, had already been inaugurated, even though the Present Age, the time of sin, rebellion and wickedness, was still proceeding apace. Saul therefore realized that his whole perspective on the way in which YHWH was going to act to unveil his plan of salvation had to be drastically rethought. He, Saul, had been ignorant of the righteousness of God, ignorant of what YHWH had been planning all along in apocalyptic fulfilment of the covenant. The death and resurrection of Jesus were themselves the great eschatological event, revealing God's covenant faithfulness, his way of putting the world to rights: the word for 'reveal' is *apokalypso*, from which of course we get 'apocalypse'. Saul was already living in the time of the end, even though the previous dimension of time was still carrying on all around him. The Present Age and the Age to Come overlapped, and he was caught in the middle, or rather, liberated in the middle, liberated to serve the same God in a new way, with a new knowledge to which he had before been blind. If the Age to Come had arrived, if the resurrection had already begun to take place, then this was the time when the Gentiles were to come in.

Saul's vision on the road to Damascus thus equipped him with an entirely new perspective, though one which kept its roots firm and deep within his previous covenantal theology. Israel's destiny had been summed up and achieved in Jesus the Messiah. The Age to Come had been inaugurated. Saul himself was summoned to be its agent. He was to declare to the pagan world that YHWH, the God of Israel, was the one true God of the whole world, and that in Jesus of Nazareth he had overcome evil and was creating a new world in which justice and peace would reign supreme.

Saul of Tarsus, in other words, had found a new vocation. It would demand all the energy, all the zeal, that he had devoted to his former way of life. He was now to be a herald of the king.

Notes

1. Quotations from the Bible throughout are the author's own translation.
2. See Acts 13:9.

CHAPTER 3

Herald of the King

We find it quite easy to separate 'conversion' from 'vocation'. The first refers to one's own experience: an inner turning or process of being turned, a deep change at the core of one's being. The second refers to one's work, what one does in public, the direction of one's outward activity. In the modern Western world it is not difficult to imagine someone being 'converted', as an inner religious experience, without a major change taking place in their 'vocation'. A non-Christian bank manager who becomes a Christian may behave differently, but will not necessarily abandon his or her original calling.

For Paul, conversion and vocation were so closely identified that it would be hard even for a razor-sharp mind like his to get a blade in between them. The manner of his conversion – stopped literally in his tracks in the hot, 'zealous' pursuit of traitors, discovering that the crucified would-be Messiah Jesus had been vindicated by God – confronted him at every level. All the things that we must suppose went on, as we would say, inside him, were matched by the total change of direction to which he was called in his outward, public life.

What never changed – this is most important to grasp once and for all – was his utter and unswerving loyalty to the God of Abraham, Isaac and Jacob, the God who made promises to Abraham, the God who gave the law, the God who spoke through the prophets. This is, of course, as controversial in current writing about Paul as it was when Paul made the same claim, as he did many times over; we shall discuss it more fully in due course. The point is that, despite what many have thought, he did not (as it were) abandon Judaism for something else. Here he, and we, are in a cleft stick. If he had abandoned Judaism and invented a new religion, he would be regarded by many as anti-Jewish. If he had claimed that Judaism's long story had reached its climax, its fulfilment, in Jesus of Nazareth, he would be regarded by many as anti-Jewish. Heads I lose; tails you win. I think he took the second route. Those who object to this on principle need to face the question, whether they would really have preferred him to take the first.

The problem, of course, is that Paul's new vocation involved him not so much in the enjoyment and propagation of a new religious experience, as in the announcement of what he saw as a public fact: that the crucified Jesus of Nazareth had been raised from the dead by Israel's God; that he had thereby been vindicated as Israel's Messiah; that, surprising though it might seem, he was therefore the Lord of the whole world. Paul's vocation was to tell this story, the true story of Israel's God and his people, the true story (in consequence) of the creator and the cosmos. And his calling was to tell it to the whole world. Nor was he simply, like Coleridge's Ancient Mariner, to go around making people sadder and wiser by telling them a long, rambling tale that said far more about the teller than the hearers. He was to go into all the world as a herald of the king.

He was, in other words – as he says several times – 'entrusted with the gospel'. But what precisely did he mean by 'the gospel'? This question takes us to the very heart of what he really said, and we must step back for a moment and look at the question quite carefully.

Misunderstanding 'Gospel' in the Modern Church

The word 'gospel', like Paul himself, has had a chequered career in the course of Christian history. During the first century, it could refer both to a message proclaimed by word of mouth and to a book about Jesus of Nazareth. In more recent times it has been used to denote a particular sort of religious meeting (a 'gospel rally'), and as a metaphor for utterly reliable information ('gospel truth'). Many Christians today, when reading the New Testament, never question what the word means, but assume that, since they know from their own context what they mean by 'the gospel', Paul and the others must have meant exactly the same thing. Everybody who knows anything about the word knows that it means 'good news'; but what sort of good news?

The word 'gospel' and the phrase 'the gospel' have come to denote, especially in certain circles within the church, something that in older theology would be called an *ordo salutis*, an order of salvation. 'The gospel' is supposed to be a description of how people get saved; of the theological mechanism whereby, in some people's language, Christ takes our sin and we his righteousness; in other people's language, Jesus becomes my personal saviour; in other languages again, I admit my sin, believe that he died for me, and commit my life to him. In many church circles, if you hear something like that, people will say that 'the gospel' has been preached. Conversely, if you hear a sermon in which the claims of Jesus Christ are related to the political or ecological questions of the day, some people will say that, well, perhaps the subject was interesting, but 'the gospel' wasn't preached.

The trouble is, of course, that though there are obviously difficult concepts in the New Testament, which send any intelligent reader off to the commentaries and dictionaries, there are others which are in fact equally difficult but which are not recognized as such. If we continue to use a word that we find in the New Testament in a sense which the New Testament itself doesn't support, that is our responsibility. But if we then seek support for *our* ideas by consulting a passage where the word occurs, we are locking ourselves in to misunderstanding the text in question, and locking ourselves out from the possibility of ever really understanding what the text actually *does* say.

In the present case, I am perfectly comfortable with what people normally *mean* when they say 'the gospel'. I just don't think it is what Paul means. In other words, I am not denying that the usual meanings are things that people ought to say, to preach about, to believe. I simply wouldn't use the word 'gospel' to denote those things.

Why not? Well, to begin with, what did 'the gospel' mean in Paul's world? Presumably his meaning cannot have been a completely private one, unrelated to what everyone else meant by the word.

Backgrounds to Paul's Usage

In order to answer this question, we must unpack it a bit. Where did the idea come from, and what echoes did the word in consequence carry both for Paul and for his readers? There have been two regular answers to this double question; Paul, after all, lived in more than one world (the Jewish, the Greek, the Roman, and so forth). I suggest that these two answers have been wrongly played off against one another, and that when we examine them both more closely we will discover that they actually belong closely together. We are here near the cutting edge of two of the central questions which, as we saw, have exercised writers on Paul for many years: how do we locate him historically, and what is the centre of his theology?

The two backgrounds regularly proposed for Paul's use of the Greek word *euangelion* ('gospel') and *euangelizesthai* ('to preach the gospel') are, predictably, the Hebrew scriptures on the one hand and pagan (Greco-Roman) usage on the other. The line between the two tends to follow the old divide between those who suppose Paul to be basically a Jewish thinker and those who see him as having borrowed his fundamental ideas from Hellenism. The evidence has been rehearsed often enough, though it is my impression that the right lessons have not always been learned from it. We must set out the main features briefly.

The Jewish usage of the relevant root include two well-known verses from Isaiah:

> Get you up to a high mountain,
> O Zion, herald of good tidings (*ho euangelizomenos Sion*);
> lift up your voice with strength,
> O Jerusalem, herald of good tidings (*ho euangelizomenos Ierousalem*);
> lift it up, do not fear;
> say to the cities of Judah,
> 'Here is your God!' (40:9)

> How beautiful upon the mountains
> are the feet of the messenger who announces peace (*hos podes euangelizomenou akoen eirenes*),
> who brings good news (*hos euangelizomenos agatha*),
> who announces salvation,
> who says to Zion, 'Your God reigns.' (52:7)

These passages, in company with others (e.g. 60:6; 61:1), are among the climactic statements of the great double theme of the whole section (Isaiah 40–66): YHWH's return to Zion and enthronement, and the return of Israel herself from her exile in Babylon. They are not simply miscellaneous 'good news', a generalized message of comfort for the downcast; they are very specific to the plight of Israel in exile. That they were read as such by at least some Jews in the second-temple period is clear from various post-biblical passages which echo or evoke them. The theme of the Isaianic herald was alive and well in the first century, as part of the great theme, which continued to be cherished by Jews at the time of Jesus and Paul (and indeed right up to our own generation): *the return of Israel from exile*. For many, if not most, Jewish writers in the second-temple period (538BC – AD70), the 'return from exile', predicted by Isaiah, Jeremiah, Ezekiel and others, had not yet taken place. This is clear, especially, in the writings from Qumran, which make explicit use, in this context, of Isaiah's figure of the 'herald'. The 'good news' or 'glad tidings' would be the message that the long-awaited release from captivity was at hand.

For some, this evidence is quite sufficient to win the verdict: this Jewish background is the context within which the New Testament 'gospel' is to be understood. Others, however, still insist upon the non-Jewish background as the vital one. In the Greek world, as is well known among scholars, *euangelion* is a regular technical term, referring to the announcement of a great victory, or to the birth, or accession, of an emperor. (The first and third of these could of course easily be combined, if someone became emperor by means of a great military victory.) The coming of a new ruler meant the promise of peace, a new start for the world, not least at the time of Augustus, who became the first Roman emperor in 31BC following a long period of civil war. An inscription from 9BC says it all:

> The providence which has ordered the whole of our life, showing concern and zeal, has ordained the most perfect consummation for human life by giving to it Augustus, by filling him with virtue for doing the work of a benefactor among men, and by sending in him, as it were, a saviour for us and those who come after us, to make war to cease, to create order everywhere...; the birthday of the god [Augustus] was the beginning for the world of the glad tidings that have come to men through him...[1]

Which of these backgrounds, then, is the appropriate one against which to read the New Testament evidence? Is 'the gospel', for Paul, an Isaianic word of comfort or an imperial proclamation?

I suggest that the antithesis between the two is a false one, based on the spurious either-or that has misleadingly divided New Testament studies for many years.

What matters in the study of words is actually not so much where an idea has *come from*, important though that is, as where it is *going to*. Confrontation is even more important than derivation. The problem is not merely that we now know that 'Jew' and 'Greek' in the first century did not live in watertight worlds (though this itself ought to make us wary of a strict either-or). It is, rather, that the Isaianic message always was about the enthronement of YHWH and the dethronement of pagan gods; about the victory of Israel and the fall of Babylon; about the arrival of the Servant King and the consequent coming of peace and justice. The scriptural message of Isaiah therefore pushes itself of its own accord into the world where pagan gods and rulers stake their claims and celebrate their enthronements. It will not do to distinguish, as is sometimes done, between supposedly 'sacred' uses (Isaiah) and supposedly 'secular' ones (Augustus). As far as first-century Jews were concerned, the 'secular' claims of the imperial cult were in fact profoundly 'religious'. The Roman world, moving fast towards the divinization of its emperors, would have eagerly agreed. And it was precisely against such 'religious' connotations – the boasting of pagan emperors from Babylon and Egypt, through the megalomania of Antiochus Epiphanes, and on to Imperial Rome – that the Jews of Paul's day had set their face. When their God, YHWH, acted within history to deliver his people, the spurious gods of the heathen would be defeated. If and when YHWH set up his own king as the true ruler, his true earthly representative, all other kingdoms would be confronted with their rightful overlord.

Once we grasp the historical setting of Paul's gospel, therefore, we discover something for which the abstract categories of traditional history-of-religions research has not prepared us. *The more Jewish we make Paul's 'gospel', the more it confronts directly the pretensions of the imperial cult, and indeed all other paganisms whether 'religious' or 'secular'.* It is because of Jewish monotheism that there can be 'no king but God'. In the history of ideas, and in lexicography, derivation is important; but so is confrontation. The all-embracing royal and religious claims of Caesar (or Babylon, or Persia, or Egypt, or Syria, or whoever) were directly challenged by the equally all-embracing claim of Israel's God. To announce that YHWH was king was to announce that Caesar is not. This was the 'good news' that Isaiah's herald was called upon to proclaim.

This, however, forces us back to our basic question. What did Paul himself mean by 'the gospel'? How did he put together this explosive combination of ideas, expectations and confrontations?

44

So, the Gospel is all about Jesus, his Kingship, his coming To the nations and the establishment of his Kingdom in hearts of men

The Fourfold Gospel Concerning Jesus

Isaiah's message was about Israel's God becoming king – king of all the world, not just of Israel. Paul's gospel was likewise a message about the one true God, the God of Israel, and his victory over all the world. In a passage that we have every reason to suppose Paul intended to be seminal both for his greatest letter – the passage stands right at its opening – and for his understanding of God, the gospel, Jesus, and his own vocation, we read:

> Paul, a servant of Messiah Jesus, called to be an apostle, set apart for the gospel of God, which he promised beforehand through his prophets in the holy scriptures – the gospel concerning his Son, who was descended from David's seed according to the flesh, and marked out as God's Son in power, according to the spirit of holiness, through the resurrection of the dead, Jesus the Messiah our Lord, through whom we have received grace and apostleship to bring about the obedience of faith among all the nations for the sake of his name... (Romans 1:1-5)

God's gospel concerning his Son. A message about God – the one true God, the God who inspired the prophets – consisting in a message about Jesus. A story – a true story – about a human life, death and resurrection through which the living God becomes king of the world. A message which had grasped Paul and, through his work, would mushroom out to all the nations. That is Paul's shorthand summary of what 'the gospel' actually is.

It is not, then, a system of how people get saved. The announcement of the gospel results in people being saved – Paul says as much a few verses later. But 'the gospel' itself, strictly speaking, is the narrative proclamation of King Jesus. He can speak equally of 'announcing the gospel' and of 'announcing Jesus', using the term *kerussein*, 'to act as a herald' in each case (e.g. 1 Corinthians 1:23; 15:12; 2 Corinthians 1:19; 4:5; 11:4; Galatians 2:2; 1 Thessalonians 2:9). When the herald makes a royal proclamation, he says 'Nero (or whoever) has become emperor.' He does not say 'If you would like to have an experience of living under an emperor, you might care to try Nero.' The proclamation is an authoritative summons to obedience – in Paul's case, to what he calls 'the obedience of faith'.

We shall come to 'faith' in due course. For the moment, we must concentrate on the actual content of the story which formed the

45

announcement made by Paul, the herald, to the world. The story of God and the world, he believed, was focused on and encapsulated within the story of Jesus of Nazareth. This story was 'gospel', good news, for all the world. I want now to outline, step by step, the core of the story as far as Paul was concerned. His announcement was that the crucified Jesus of Nazareth had been raised from the dead; that he was thereby proved to be Israel's Messiah; that he was thereby installed as Lord of the world. Or, to put it yet more compactly: Jesus, the crucified and risen Messiah, is Lord.

The crucified Jesus

It is an obvious truism to say that the cross stands at the heart of Paul's whole theology. (It is, however, revealing to see how several treatments of Paul, both at the most serious and at the more popular levels, fail to treat it as central.) The problem for anyone who attempts to think Paul's thoughts after him is that each time he mentions the cross — as he does literally dozens of times, on almost every page of his letters — he says something different about it. How has God fulfilled the promises to Abraham? Through the cross. What is at stake if unthinking ex-pagans eat meat offered to idols? They may offend a brother or sister 'for whom Christ died'. What happens in baptism? People die with Christ. How did God overthrow the rule of the evil powers? The cross was his triumphal procession. What is the supreme revelation of God's love, and hence of his unshakeable commitment to his people and his world? The death of Jesus. How are Jew and Gentile reconciled? Through the cross. Why are Christians no longer 'under the law'? Because 'they died to the law through the body of Christ'. What has God done about the seemingly all-powerful rule of sin and death? He has condemned sin on the cross, and has thereby undone the power of death. And so on. And so on.

We are in danger of being lulled by this constant refrain into insensibility to what Paul was actually saying — and, equally importantly, was heard to be saying in the world of his day. Crucifixes regularly appear as jewellery in today's post-Christian Western world, and the wearers are often blissfully unaware that their pretty ornament depicts the ancient equivalent, all in one, of the hangman's noose, the electric chair, the thumbscrew, and the rack. Or, to be more precise, something which combined all four but went far beyond them; crucifixion was such an utterly horrible thing that the very word was usually avoided in polite Roman society. Every time Paul spoke of it – especially when he spoke in the same breath of salvation, love, grace and freedom – he and his hearers must have been conscious of the slap in the face thereby administered to their normal expectations and sensibilities. Somehow, we need to remind ourselves of this every time Paul mentions Jesus' death, especially the mode of that death.

When we attempt this exercise, it is precisely the slap in the face that gets to the point. God has reversed the world's values. He has done the impossible. He has turned shame into glory and glory into shame. His is the folly that outsmarts the wise, the weakness that overpowers the strong. The cross is for Paul the symbol, as it was the means, of the liberating victory of the one true God, the creator of the world, over all the enslaving powers that have usurped his authority. That is why it is at the heart of 'the gospel'. Isaiah spoke of a herald with a 'gospel' message; as his prophecy developed, emphasizing the victory of Israel's God over all the idols of Babylon, it contained at its heart the strange picture of the servant of YHWH, suffering and being vindicated. The world of Paul's audience knew of 'the gospel' as a message about someone, most likely a king or emperor, who had won a great victory, perhaps thereby attaining the throne. Paul, with both feet planted firmly in the prophets, addressed the pagan world with the news of a new king, a new emperor, a new Lord.

For this reason I suggest that we give priority – a priority among equals, perhaps, but still a priority – to those Pauline expressions of the crucifixion of Jesus which describe it as the decisive victory over the 'principalities and powers'. Nothing in the many other expressions of the meaning of the cross is lost if we put this in the centre. The announcement of 'the crucified Messiah' is the key to everything because it declares to the rulers of this age that their time is up; had they realized what was going on, 'they would not have crucified the Lord of glory' (1 Corinthians 1:18 – 2:8). Contrary to what casual onlookers might have thought, when Jesus was crucified it was he who was leading the principalities and powers in his triumphal procession, celebrating *his* victory over *them*, instead of the other way around (Colossians 2:14-15). The death of Jesus had the effect of liberating both Jew and Gentile from the enslaving force of the 'elements of the world' (Galatians 4:1-11). And, towering over almost everything else, the death of Jesus, seen as the culmination of his great act of obedience, is the means whereby the reign of sin and death is replaced with the reign of grace and righteousness (Romans 5:12-21). 'The gospel' is indeed the announcement of a royal victory.

When we ask how it was that Jesus' cruel death was the decisive victory over the powers, sin and death included, Paul at once replies: because it was the fulfilment of God's promise that through Abraham and his seed he would undo the evil in the world. God established his covenant with Abraham in the first place for this precise purpose. That is why, in the great sweeping argument of the letter to the Romans, Paul's exposition of God's faithfulness to his covenant (in technical language, his 'righteousness'), is explained in terms of the fulfilment of the promises to Abraham (3:21 – 4:25), and then explored in terms of the undoing of Adam's sin (5:12-21) and ultimately of the liberation of the whole creation (8:17-25). The same sequence of thought may be observed in various other places. In Galatians the full exposition of the covenant with Abraham, and how it has reached its dramatic climax in Jesus Christ, points ahead to the message of 'new creation' (6:15). In 2 Corinthians, similarly, new covenant (chapter 3) leads to new creation (chapter 5). And always the fulfilment focuses on the death of Jesus, the covenant-fulfilling act, the moment when God executed judicial sentence on sin itself (Romans 3:24-26; 8:3), the moment when God's astonishing love was unveiled in all its glory (Romans 5:6-11; 8:31-39).

This is fulfilment; not abrogation. It would be fatally easy to suppose that Paul acquired on the road to Damascus, or in his thinking soon after, a scheme of thought, focused on the cross, which made him want to abandon everything Jewish, including the sense that Israel's God was going to fulfil his promises at last. It would be possible (though very misleading) to read Philippians 3:7-8 in that sense – 'I have suffered the loss of all things, and count them as so much rubbish, so that I may gain Christ'. Not so. It is certainly true that neither Paul nor any of his Jewish contemporaries had expected their God to act in anything like this way. But Paul's understanding of the death of Jesus was not a brand new idea appearing from nowhere. The power of his 'gospel' came precisely from the fact that it addressed the pagan world with the full weight of Jewish history and tradition behind it. Saul the Pharisee would have read the Jewish scriptures not least as a lament for all that had gone wrong – for Israel's failure and disloyalty, for her sin and rebellion, for the consequent national disasters, defeat, subjugation and exile. Read Psalm 74 (for instance), and imagine Saul of Tarsus praying it fervently in the Temple courtyard, under the eye of Roman guards watching from their fortress.

Israel's fate, in other words – the suffering at the hands of the pagans – had not been swept aside. It was not irrelevant. It had reached its climax precisely in the death of Jesus, the representative Messiah of Israel. When Paul declared that 'the Messiah died for our sins according to the scriptures' – this, by the way, is the beginning of his official summary of 'the gospel' in 1 Corinthians 15:3-8 – he does not mean that he can find half a dozen 'proof-texts' from scripture that he can cunningly twist into predictions of the crucifixion. He means that the entire scriptural story, the great drama of God's dealings with Israel, came together when the young Jew from Nazareth was nailed up by the Romans and left to die. Though we have here only glanced at a small fraction of what Paul says about the cross, we have said enough to make the point: the shameful death of Jesus at the hands of the pagans was, for Paul, the centre and starting-point of what 'the gospel' was all about. It was the fulfilment of the Isaianic message. It was the proclamation of the ultimate royal victory. It was the Jewish message of good news for the world.

But (someone might say) hundreds of Jews, young and old, were crucified by the Romans in the first century. Why was this execution so special? Paul's answer would have been twofold. This crucifixion was different because of who it was that was crucified, and because of what happened next. We shall take these in the reverse order: Jesus' resurrection, his Messiahship, and the fact that he is therefore Lord of the world. Together with the crucifixion, these constitute the basic elements of Paul's 'gospel'.

The risen Jesus

'If Christ is not raised, our proclamation is empty and so is your faith; if Christ is not raised, your faith is futile and you are still in your sins' (1 Corinthians 15:14, 17). Without the resurrection, the crucifixion carries no gospel, no announcement of royal victory, and hence no consequences of salvation. But that doesn't mean that the cross is just a messy interlude prior to the real victory. As we have just seen, Paul understands Jesus' execution as the moment when the creator's love wins the victory over the rebellious creation, when the forces that have enslaved humans and the world are defeated once and for all. Yet, to continue this theological see-saw process, if that victory did not lead directly to Jesus' own resurrection, it did not happen at all. Paul, in line with a major theme throughout the Bible, understood sin and death as bound together in a tight nexus. If Jesus had defeated sin, death could not hold him. If (conversely) he rose again from the dead, it meant he had indeed dealt with sin on the cross – in other words, that God had achieved at last what he had promised to Abraham and the prophets. That is how Paul's logic works in the first nineteen verses of 1 Corinthians 15, a deliberate set-piece exposition of Paul's 'gospel'.

Everything thus hinges on Jesus' resurrection. Scholars and popular writers often make a great song and dance about what Paul thought was about to happen in the future, as though his 'eschatological' or 'apocalyptic' beliefs had to do with events yet to occur. As far as Paul was concerned, the most important eschatological event, through which the living God had unveiled (or, if you like, 'apocalypsed') his plan to save the whole cosmos, *had occurred when Jesus rose from the dead*. He wasn't just living in the last days. He was living in the *first* days – of a whole new world order. As with the cross, the resurrection permeates Paul's thinking and writing; and it isn't by any means just the future resurrection, to which of course Paul looks forward. It is the resurrection of Jesus, to which he looks back.

It is vital to grasp that for a Pharisee of Paul's background and training the resurrection meant, inalienably and incontestably, the *bodily* resurrection. 1 Corinthians 15 rules out two possible ways of understanding the resurrection. On the one hand, Paul didn't see it as simply the resuscitation of a corpse. Jesus didn't return into the same mode of physical existence as he had lived before. On the other hand, Paul didn't see it as the abandonment of Jesus' physical body. If you had suggested to him that 'the resurrection' might have occurred while the tomb of Jesus was still occupied by his corpse, he wouldn't just have disagreed; he would have suggested that you didn't understand what the relevant words meant. First-century Jews held a variety of beliefs about what God would do with, or to, his people after their death. But 'resurrection' was never a term covering lots of different options on that score. It had to do, specifically, with re-embodiment, with a new physical existence. When Paul talks about a 'spiritual body' (1 Corinthians 15:44), he doesn't mean 'spiritual' in the Platonic sense, i.e. non-material. He means a *body* (physical, in some sense), which is *constituted* by 'spirit'.

Paul believed, in fact, that Jesus had gone *through* death *and out the other side*. Jesus had gone into a new mode of physicality, for which there was no precedent and of which there was, as yet, no other example. And this too had happened 'according to the scriptures' (1 Corinthians 15:4). Once again, this doesn't mean that Paul could dig out a handful of biblical proof-texts predicting that someone would rise again as an isolated event within history. It means that he saw the entire biblical narrative moving this way.

'Resurrection' was, in Ezekiel 37, a metaphor for the return of Israel from exile. When Paul was faced with the fact of Jesus' resurrection, he concluded that the return from exile had in fact happened. Exile had reached its height in Jesus' death; now he had come through death, through the ultimate exile, and was set free not just from Greece or Rome, from Herod, Pilate and Caiaphas, but from sin and death, the ultimate enemies (1 Corinthians 15:25-6). This meant that the Age to Come, the Eschaton of Jewish expectation, had already arrived, even though it didn't look like Paul had expected. It meant that Israel had in principle been redeemed, in the person of her anointed representative. It meant that the Gentiles were now to be summoned to join Israel in celebrating the new day, the day of deliverance.

It meant, too, that the Age to Come, for which Israel had longed, was arriving *in two stages*. In 1 Corinthians 15 Paul reworks the more or less traditional model of a Jewish apocalypse, making it clear that the end *has* already happened (in Jesus' resurrection) and that the end *is still* to happen (when all Jesus' people are raised to life). In Romans 8 he amplifies this, and broadens its scope: Jesus' resurrection is the guarantee of the future liberation from death and corruption not only of all those who are 'in Christ' but of creation as a whole. Paul is conscious of living between the End (Mark One) and the End (Mark Two). This is the real novelty in his theology. But it remains a novelty which arises within his Pharisaic Judaism, not by abandoning that frame of reference and getting a new one from somewhere else.

It meant, directly and most importantly, that despite his shameful crucifixion – which, by itself, would have meant the shattering of any messianic aspirations he might have had – Jesus of Nazareth really was Israel's Messiah, the true, God-given, anointed king.

King Jesus

'Christ' is not a name. It is a title. It *becomes* a name (denoting somebody, but without extra connotation), at some point in early Christianity, as its Jewish meaning is forgotten by Gentile converts. Equally, 'Christ' in the first century does not mean 'a divine being'. That, too, is a later development (as we shall see, Paul thought Jesus was divine; but the word 'Christ' did not express, perhaps could not have expressed, that belief). 'Christ', for Paul, means 'Messiah'. And 'Messiah', of course, means 'the anointed one'.

Where this is ignored (as it often is in both scholarly and popular writing) we should not be surprised to find that a good many Pauline passages remain stubbornly opaque.

That phrase could denote other people; a priest, for instance. But its major referent in first-century Judaism was the coming king. Scholars sometimes write about Jewish expectations of a Messiah on the basis of literary speculations at the time. Sometimes, in this process, even 'Messiah' can sound somewhat 'religious', removed from actual first-century life. We know, mostly from the pages of Josephus, of a dozen or more messianic or would-be messianic movements within a hundred years either side of Jesus. This is the atmosphere we need to breathe if we want to understand what Paul is talking about. He believed that Jesus was the true king. An unexpected king, yes. A king who turned everything, including expectations of what the coming king would do and be, upside down, yes. But the true king nonetheless. The resurrection proved it. To remind ourselves of this it would do no harm from time to time to translate *Iesous Christos* not as 'Jesus Christ', nor even as 'Jesus the Messiah', but as 'King Jesus'.

Paul's 'gospel' is therefore 'the gospel of Christ': not so much a message which is the property of the king, as a message whose subject is the king. It is through this king that the true God has made himself known. Paul's preaching of the gospel involved him in portraying Jesus Christ publicly as the crucified one (Galatians 3:1). For Paul, the reason why there is good news at all is that in and through the cross of King Jesus the one true God has dealt decisively with evil. The prisoners can only be comforted if it is true that the jailor has himself been locked up. Zion can only receive truly good news if it is true that Babylon has been defeated. At the heart of Paul's gospel there stands the claim that the death of Jesus the king has defeated evil at its very heart.

The claim that Paul regarded Jesus as the king, the Messiah, and that he announced him as such, is controversial within New Testament scholarship at present, and I want, in explaining why I make this claim, to show how the logic of it works in practice.

Let us return to Romans 1:3-4, where, as we saw, Paul introduces himself and his letter with a brief and pithy formula (see above, page 45). Generations of scholars, determined to resist the idea that Paul thought of Jesus in any way as the king, the Messiah, the true Son of David, have of course allowed this passage to drop off the front of Romans, as they hurried on to what they took to be the real introductory formula in verses

16-17, the announcement of the righteousness of God (about which I shall have more to say later). They then dismiss verses 3 and 4 as a 'traditional formula' which Paul is quoting to put his audience at rest, even though he himself does not regard it as an accurate summary of his thinking. But it is absurd to suppose that Paul, who regularly uses his opening formulae to introduce the major subject-matter of his letters, should have slipped in such a carefully worded formula at such a crucial place in such a vital letter if it does not in fact represent not only what he thinks in general but what he intends to say in what follows. The latter point is clearly impossible to prove without going through a detailed exegesis of Romans; but I hope at least to point out ways in which we can see this royal theology at the heart of Paul's whole thought.

The formula, which Paul explicitly designates as his 'gospel', speaks of the Son of David. We know from a good many Jewish sources, not least Qumran, that Davidic sonship was central to some ideas at least of Messiahship; and we know at least one or two of the scriptural texts which were regularly adduced to support the point. Perhaps the best known is 2 Samuel 7. In Nathan's oracle to David, God promises David that he will build him a 'house': when David dies, God will raise up his seed after him, who will sit on his throne, and (God says) 'I will be to him a father, and he shall be to me a son.' This promise is celebrated in the later version of the same incident in Chronicles, and of course in two royal psalms in particular, Psalms 2 and 89. All these passages appear in various Jewish traditions of speculation about the coming Messiah.

When, therefore, Paul tells us that the gospel he preaches is the one promised beforehand in holy scripture, and that its central figure is one who was from the seed of David and is now marked out as Son of God, we would have to imitate Lord Nelson, putting a blind eye to the telescope, to deny that Paul intends to evoke precisely this collocation of scriptural themes, which is about as well attested in Jewish literature as any collection of messianic ideas. He is, in other words, announcing a gospel which is not just a message about the availability of salvation, which happens to have been achieved by someone called 'Jesus', whose other name (for Paul) is 'Christ'. He is announcing that the messianic promises of salvation have come true in Jesus. Jesus is the king, not only of Israel but of all the world. When Paul proceeds at once to say exactly this in verse 5 – which states clearly enough that God has sent Paul to summon all the nations to allegiance to this King Jesus – we should not doubt that it is this messianic concept which he has in mind. And when, later in the letter, we meet again and again the sense that the promises made to Abraham and his family have come true in this Jesus – that Jesus has offered God the obedience and faithfulness which should have characterized Israel but did not; that he is the Messiah from Israel according to the flesh, and now also Lord of all the world – then we have initial justification in saying that Romans 1:3-4 does indeed provide the thematic launching-pad for the letter's deepest argument. Paul's theology in Romans is, at its heart, royal.

So, I suggest, is his theology in Galatians. We may consider briefly the long argument which runs from the start of Galatians 3:1 to 4:11. This is all about the way in which the promises to Abraham have been fulfilled precisely 'in Christ', in the Messiah. There are many Jewish texts in which the historical sequence of thought, in answer to the question 'how will God be true to his promises to Abraham?', reaches its answer and fulfilment as 'in the Son of David, the Messiah'. Are there indications, in addition to the high concentration of the word *Christos* at precisely these points of the chapter, that Paul may have had this sequence of thought in mind?

The answer is Yes. Central to his argument is the idea of the 'seed': the true seed of Abraham, the fulfilment of the promises. As several scholars have shown, this provides a natural link to a whole collection of messianic promises which grow out of the Nathan oracle we mentioned a moment ago, in which the Messiah is the 'seed of David'. And, at one crucial turning-point in the argument, Paul alludes to another of the best-known messianic promises, that in Genesis 49:10.

The promise, much quoted and studied by Jews in the second-temple period, is difficult to translate, but it was certainly understood at the time to mean 'The sceptre shall not depart from Judah until he comes whose right it is' – in other words, the royal house of Judah will continue until it finds its fulfilment in the Messiah. The critical phrase 'until he comes', and the sense of a long waiting after which the promises will be fulfilled, is what we find in Galatians 3:19: the law was given, because of transgressions, *until he comes, the 'seed' to whom the promise was made*. Within his overall argument about Abraham, Paul is operating with an implicit royal theology and exegesis. We then find, in increasing concentration in the rest of the chapter, usage of *Christos* which, as I have argued elsewhere, can best be explained in terms of 'incorporation into the people of the Messiah': he describes Christians as 'baptized into Christ', 'putting on Christ', 'one in Christ', and 'belonging to Christ' (3:27-29). The only way we can avoid reading the entire argument messianically is if, once again, we employ the method of Lord Nelson.

Galatians 3 then leads straight into Galatians 4, in which Paul uses explicitly messianic language to describe Jesus. He is the lord and heir of all things; he is the Son of God (a royal title, remember, in Psalms 2 and 89); he is the one through whom the pagan nations are brought into submission, and the true people of God liberated. Through his coming and work the true God has finally been revealed. The 'gospel of God' is thus indeed 'the gospel of God concerning his Son'. For Paul, 'the gospel' is the story of Jesus of Nazareth, crucified and risen, seen as King Jesus, the promised Messiah of Israel.

Jesus is Lord

The final step in Paul's gospel narrative was to assert of Jesus what the Psalmist asserted of the true Davidic king:

> I will tell of the decree of the LORD:
>   He said to me, 'You are my Son;
>   today I have begotten you.
> Ask of me, and I will make the nations your heritage,
>   and the ends of the earth your possession.' (Psalm 2:7-8)

> Give the king your justice, O God,
>   and your righteousness to the king's son...
> May he have dominion from sea to sea,
>   and from the River to the ends of the earth. (Psalm 72:1, 8)

> I have found my servant David;
>   with my holy oil I have anointed him;
> my hand shall always remain with him;
>   my arm also shall strengthen him...
> He shall cry to me: 'You are my Father,
>   my God, and the Rock of my salvation!'
> I will make him the firstborn,
>   the highest of the kings of the earth.
> (Psalm 89:19-20, 26-27)

In other words, the coming King of the Jews will also be the king of all the earth. This, of course, is simply the leading edge of the doctrine of election, the choice of Israel as the one people of the one true God: if Israel is the people through whom God will address the whole world, Israel's king will be the focal point of that action. The Messiah will be Lord, not only of Israel, but also of the whole world.

This is precisely what Paul says of Jesus:

> There is no distinction between Jew and Greek, for the same Lord is Lord of all, rich in mercy to all who call upon him. (Romans 10:12)

Paul uses the title 'Lord' for Jesus so frequently that the uses take up several columns in a small-print concordance. Like *Christos*, though, the word *Kyrios* ('Lord'), is often taken for granted, or even (perhaps as a result of its over-use in popular devotional address to God or Jesus) downgraded into almost another mere name, denoting Jesus but not saying anything much about him. It is vital, if we want to understand all the dimensions of Paul's gospel, that we reclaim the full significance of this heavily freighted word.

Like 'gospel' itself, 'Lord' carries two apparently quite different meanings, depending on whether you look towards Paul's Jewish upbringing or his Greco-Roman audience. In the present section I shall concentrate on the latter; but in the next chapter – which is really an extension of the present one, though its topic is so large and important that it needs space of its own – I shall draw out further the significance of the former.

In the Greco-Roman world around which Paul moved so widely, and which formed the primary audience for his message, the word *Kyrios* could refer to all sorts of people. It could sometimes simply be a polite form of address, like the English 'Sir'. But, just as the polite English 'Sir' does not rule out the stricter sense, used to address a knight, so in Paul's world *Kyrios* was regularly used, not merely for polite address to a social superior, but to denote *the* social superior above all: the emperor. Ultimately, for the Roman point of view, there was only one Lord of the world. According to Paul, he now had a rival.

Luke makes this point clearly enough, when (despite what many think of as his desire to defend Paul against the charge of being a seditious trouble-maker) he has him brought before the magistrates in Thessalonica on a charge of saying that 'there is another king, named Jesus' (Acts 17:7). It is hard to imagine Luke inventing this charge.

In fact, Paul in his letters was saying more or less exactly the same thing. In a famous passage, Philippians 2:5-11 (which we shall look at in more detail in the next chapter), Paul is not simply articulating a breathtaking vision of who Jesus is, and indeed of who God is. He is also, quite directly and explicitly, subverting the claims of the other great would-be lord of the world of his day, namely Caesar. 'Every tongue' he writes, 'shall confess that "Jesus is Lord", to the glory of God the Father.' As with 'gospel', so with 'Lord': Paul's language is borrowed not only from Isaiah, but also from the imperial cult. In several texts from the Roman empire, we find formulaic phrases, referring to the emperor's accession, in which the sequence of thought runs as follows. Such-and-such a person (Augustus, Nero, or whoever) has been a good servant of the state, perhaps by winning some great victory; we therefore hail him as our lord, and entrust ourselves to him to be our saviour. We hail him as *Kyrios*, and trust him to be our *Soter*.

Paul, writing to the Philippian church (Philippi was, of course, a Roman colony), cannot but have been aware of the implications of what he was saying. Indeed, I think it is likely that this is part of his real message to the Philippian church: don't be lulled into thinking that you can serve two masters, that there are two Lords of the world. There is only one, and that is Jesus. 'Every tongue shall confess that Jesus is Lord'; then, at the climactic end of the next chapter, 'Our citizenship is in heaven; and from there we await the Saviour, the Lord Jesus Christ... who has the power to submit all things to himself' (Philippians 3:20-21). Paul's gospel was indeed a royal announcement. He had not left behind the category of kingship when he went out, away from the Jewish world, to preach to the Gentiles. That, on the contrary, was the context where the specifically Jewish message of the gospel really began to bite. 'Another king' – as Paul knew only too well, people tend to get put in prison for saying that sort of thing. We should not be surprised to discover that that was where Paul was when he wrote half of his letters.

The Gospel of God

We have studied Paul's 'gospel', and have seen that underneath his regular formulae ('the Lord Jesus Christ' and so on) there is a carefully worked out sequence of thought, an implicit story-line, which when properly understood reveals that he both remained totally rooted in his Jewish world and was aiming his message directly at the principalities and powers of the Roman world, from Caesar downwards. Ultimately, though, this message was not simply a message about Jesus. Everything he said about Jesus was, for him, a way of talking about God.

In the world Paul was addressing, the word 'God' (*Theos* in Greek, *Deus* in Latin) was a question mark. People wrote books about whether God, or the gods, existed, and if so what he, she, it or they were like, what they did, whether they interfered in ordinary mortal lives, and so on. Almost everybody took the gods mildly seriously; hardly anybody took them very seriously. In the world Paul had come from, however, there was only one God. He was the creator of the world; he was also the God of Israel. And almost everybody took him very seriously indeed.

Every loyal Jew believed, moreover, that one day the wider world, as well, would have to take the God of Israel seriously. He would establish his kingdom over all the world. He would reveal that Israel had been his special people all along. He would condemn the world for its idolatry and immorality. This is the point of a book such as the Wisdom of Solomon, written roughly at the time of Jesus and Paul. If Saul of Tarsus had felt called, as a Pharisee, to preach to the Gentiles, this would have been part of his stock-in-trade, coupled with an invitation to worship the true God, the God of Israel, and to take on the Jewish way of life, the Torah.

The 'gospel' of Paul the apostle was also a message about God, the one God of Israel, the creator of the world. It, too, was a summons to reject pagan idolatry and to turn to the true God, the source of life and all good things. Paul summarizes this message in the first chapter of what some hold to be his first surviving letter, namely 1 Thessalonians. And we see in several other passages how he viewed the effect of his preaching. Consider, first, Galatians 4:1-11.

> [1] What I mean is this. So long as the heir is a minor, he is no different from a slave, even if he is master of everything; [2] but he is under guardians and overseers until the time set by the father. [3] So with us: when we were in our minority, we were enslaved under the 'elements of the world'; [4] but when the fulness of the time arrived, God sent forth his Son, born of a woman, born under the law, [5] so that he might redeem those who were under the law, so that we might receive adoption as children. [6] And because you are his children, God has sent forth the Spirit of his Son into our hearts, crying 'Abba, Father!' [7] So you are no longer a slave, but a child; and if a child, then an heir through God.
>
> [8] When you formerly did not know God, we were enslaved to beings that by nature are not gods. [9] But now that you have come to

know God – or rather, to be known by God – how can you turn back again to the weak and poverty-stricken 'elements' to whom you want to be enslaved again? [10] You are observing special days, months, seasons and years! [11] I am afraid for you, afraid that I may have wasted my time in my work with you.

This passage stands at a climactic moment in the whole letter, drawing together the argument of the preceding chapter and laying the foundations for what is to come. It may thus fairly be seen as a summary of 'the gospel' which is so clearly stated as a main theme in the opening section of the letter. Verses 1-7 state in one particular form the content of 'the gospel' which Paul preached: 'when the time had fully come, God sent forth his Son, born of a woman, born under the law, to redeem those who were under the law'. Verses 8-11 describe substantially the context and effect of that gospel-preaching: formerly the Galatians did not 'know God', but now – as a result of Paul's preaching about Jesus – they have come to know God – 'or rather, to be known by God' (4:9). The passage, in other words, spells out in more detail the challenge which Paul throws down in 1:6-9: how can the Galatians turn away from the true gospel to a pseudo-gospel, a human invention, a parody of the truth?

According to 4:1-11, the message of the Pauline gospel is this: the true God has sent his Son, in fulfilment of the prophecies of scripture, to redeem his people from their bondage to false gods, the 'elements of the world' (4:3, 9). He now sends his own spirit to make his people truly what they were before only in theory and hope – his own children, heirs of his world. Equipped with this gospel, the Galatian Christians now *know the true God*, and are known by him. That is, they have received the great blessing promised by Isaiah throughout chapters 40–55. The one true God has revealed himself in saving them, routing the idols of the nations in doing so.

This message of good news, with the cross of Jesus at its very heart, decisively confronts the power of the spurious gods. The God now revealed in the sending of the Son and the spirit (4:1-7) is the God beside whom the defeated principalities and powers pale into insignificance (4:8-11). The 'gospel' is for Paul, at its very heart, *an announcement about the true God as opposed to the false gods*. This announcement was, and Paul expected it to be, controversial. The riot in Ephesus (referred to in Acts 19) was not entirely a misunderstanding. If Paul's message was true, the makers of idols were right to perceive him as a threat.

There is a good deal more to say about what Paul meant by the word 'God'. But in order to say it we shall need to dig deeper to the very heart of Paul's gospel, and this will take another chapter to do. If the gospel was both the message about Jesus and the message about God, what was the relationship, in Paul's mind, between Jesus and God?

Conclusion

Before we can move to this question, some words of conclusion about Paul's gospel. My proposal has been that 'the gospel' is not, for Paul, a message about 'how one gets saved', in an individual and ahistorical sense. It is a fourfold announcement about Jesus:

1. In Jesus of Nazareth, specifically in his cross, the decisive victory has been won over all the powers of evil, including sin and death themselves.

2. In Jesus' resurrection the New Age has dawned, inaugurating the long-awaited time when the prophecies would be fulfilled, when Israel's exile would be over, and the whole world would be addressed by the one creator God.

3. The crucified and risen Jesus was, all along, Israel's Messiah, her representative king.

4. Jesus was therefore also the Lord, the true king of the world, the one at whose name every knee would bow.

It is, moreover, a double and dramatic announcement about God:

1. The God of Israel is the one true God, and the pagan deities are mere idols.

2. The God of Israel is now made known in and through Jesus himself.

Each aspect of this announcement is, I believe, vital if we are to understand what Paul means by 'gospel' at all. It is because Paul sees his Galatian opponents failing to grasp this whole sequence of thought that he accuses them of being seduced by 'another gospel'. It is because Paul wants his Roman readers to get things as clear as possible before he arrives there that he writes his greatest (and densest) letter, a letter which, by being all about Jesus, is even more so all about God.

The 'gospel', then, is, as Paul says in Romans 1:16, 'the power of God for salvation'. The word for 'power' here is *dynamis*, from which we get 'dynamite'. To understand Paul's meaning, we may invoke a further technical term. Paul speaks in Acts (20:24) of 'the gospel of the grace of God'. But what is grace? Grace is not a 'thing' – a heavenly gas, a pseudo-substance, which can be passed to and fro or pumped down pipelines. The word 'grace' is a shorthand way of speaking about God himself, the God who loves totally and unconditionally, whose love overflows in self-giving in creation, in redemption, in rooting out evil and sin and death from his world, in bringing to life that which was dead. Paul's gospel reveals this God in all his grace, all his love.

But it doesn't just reveal all this so that people can admire it from a distance. It reveals it precisely by putting it into action. The royal proclamation is not simply the conveying of true information about the kingship of Jesus. It is the putting into effect of that kingship, the decisive and authoritative summoning to allegiance. Paul discovered, at the heart of his missionary practice, that when he announced the lordship of Jesus Christ, the sovereignty of King Jesus, this very announcement was the means by which the living God reached out with his love and changed the hearts and lives of men and women, forming them into a community of love across traditional barriers, liberating them from the paganism which had held them captive, enabling them to become, for the first time, the truly human beings they were meant to be. The gospel, Paul would have said, is not just about God's power saving people. It *is* God's power at work to save people.

When Paul announced this gospel message, it carried its own weight, its own authority, quite independently of the rhetorical or linguistic skill of the herald. But if the heralding of this gospel was the authoritative summons to allegiance, it could not but pose a challenge to all other 'powers' that claimed human loyalty. That is why to retain, or to embrace, symbols and praxis which spoke of other loyalties and other allegiances was to imply that other powers were still being invoked. And that, according to Paul, was to deny 'the truth of the gospel'.

Paul, then, had grasped the truth: the one true God was now made known in Jesus (and in the Spirit). And, grasping that, he knew that he was himself grasped, held, sustained and saved by the faithful love of the faithful God. Being so grasped, he found himself 'a servant of Christ, set apart for God's gospel'; in proclaiming this gospel, he discovered again and again that it was indeed God's power for salvation.

But this argument simply brings us back to the question I highlighted a moment ago, to which we can now turn at last. If God is the king, and if Jesus is the king, what is the relation, in Paul's mind at least, between God and Jesus?

Notes

1. The inscription was found in Priene on the Asia Minor coast: *Priene Inscriptions*, edited by F. Hiller von Gärtringen, 105, 40.

CHAPTER 4

Paul and Jesus

In one sense, this whole book is of course about Paul and Jesus. But we must now tackle head on the question: what did Paul think, at the deepest level, about Jesus? Did he think he was divine? If so, why, and how did he express it?

I shall argue in this chapter that Paul did indeed think that Jesus was divine, and that — contrary to much repeated assertion, both among scholars and at a more popular level — he did so *without leaving for a moment the home base of Jewish monotheism*. To make this case I must first explain in more detail how first-century Jews thought of the one true God.

First-Century Jewish Monotheism

Jewish monotheism in this period was not an inner analysis of the being of the one true God. It was not an attempt at describing numerically what this God is, so to speak, on the inside. Instead, it made two claims, both of them polemical in their historical context. On the one hand, Jewish monotheism asserted that the one God, the God of Israel, was the only God of the whole world; that therefore the pagan gods and goddesses were blasphemous nonsenses; that the pagan world, worshipping these idols, was inherently sinful; and that the true God would one day decisively defeat these pagan gods and their powers, and vindicate Israel as his true people. Monotheism, in short, was a fighting doctrine. It was what sustained the Maccabees in their successful battle against Antiochus Epiphanes. It was what sustained the great Rabbi Akiba in his unsuccessful fight against the emperor Hadrian.

On the other hand, Jewish monotheism contained the strong assertion that the dualists were wrong. The material world was not the evil creation of an evil god. There was only one God, and he was ultimately responsible for the way the world was. That responsibility implied, of course, that he would take steps to save, heal and restore it. Once again, therefore, monotheism was a fighting doctrine; one could not sit back and dismiss the rest of the world as evil, knowing one was going to escape it altogether sooner or later. Jewish-style monotheism committed its adherents both to the effort to bring in the kingdom within the physical world (though Jews differed as to how much effort was appropriate) and to the belief that those who died ahead of the time would be raised physically to life when the great day came. Rejecting dualism, the monotheist was committed to bodily resurrection.

Within this monotheism, many Jews were very flexible about how they spoke of this one true God acting within the world, and especially in relation to Israel. They used a range of language, in what sometimes seems today a quite bewildering fashion, to suggest that this God was near to his people, and was active in a variety of ways within the world.

There are five language-sets in particular which they employed for this purpose. Briefly, they are as follows: Wisdom, Torah, Spirit, Word and Shekinah (the last is the technical term for the presence of the true God 'tabernacling' with his people, living in the Temple in Jerusalem as he lived in the tent of meeting in the wilderness). Sometimes some of these are closely identified with each other, as in Ben-Sira (Ecclesiasticus) 24. The point to be grasped here is that the Jews did not conceive of their one true God as a long way away, either from them or from the world at large. He was, of course, transcendent; he couldn't be contained within the world. But he was not detached. When he acted within the world, he didn't intervene from a great distance. He was always present, always active. Sometimes his actions took one by surprise.

In particular, as should be clear after the previous chapter, Jewish monotheism set its face firmly against emperor-worship. The claims of the Roman emperors, especially in the Eastern mediterranean where emperor-worship caught on earlier than in Rome itself, were absolute and all-embracing. This made sense, within the Roman worldview; after all, if Augustus ruled the entire known world, did not that mean that he was, in some sense or other, a supreme god? But the Jews knew that there was only one supreme God. Their claim could not, ultimately, be set alongside those of the emperors as two claims among many. Both sides knew it.

They maintained an uneasy *modus vivendi*. But thirty years or so after Jesus' death, the explosion came. The Jewish war was not simply a clash between a recalcitrant rebel subject and a mighty imperial power. It was a clash between two competing worldviews. Ultimately, there cannot be two Lords of the world. As far as the Romans were concerned, their victory in AD70 proved their point. As far as the Jews were concerned, the fall of Jerusalem merely heightened the problem of adhering to their monotheism, and fuelled further revolt.

So much, so briefly, for Jewish beliefs about the one true God. I now wish to argue that Paul took precisely this Jewish doctrine and redefined it – with Jesus, and the Spirit, within it.

Jesus Within Paul's Jewish Monotheism

One of the most striking things about Pauline Christology – Paul's statements about Jesus – is this: at the very moment when he is giving Jesus the highest titles and honours, he is also emphasizing that he, Paul, is a good Jewish-style monotheist. Faced with this evidence, we either have to conclude that Paul was really a very muddled theologian indeed, or that he intended to say, as clearly as was open to him, that when he put Jesus and God in the same bracket he was not intending to add a second god to the pantheon, as in paganism. Nor was he intending that Jesus be seen as somehow absorbed into the being of the one God, without remainder. He was inviting his readers to see Jesus as retaining his full identity as the man Jesus of Nazareth, but within the inner being of the one God, the God of Jewish monotheism.

There are three passages where this is particularly striking. The first is 1 Corinthians 8:1-6. Here Paul is sketching out, with great pastoral sensitivity, the way through one of the many problems the Corinthian church faced, as they struggled to make sense of their new identity in the face of their strongly pagan surroundings. What should they do about meat that had been offered in sacrifice in the temple of an idol? This was no side-issue; virtually all meat available in a town like Corinth would have gone that route. Idol-temples and restaurants were usually one and the same place. To refuse idol-meat might well mean remaining vegetarian.

Paul begins the chapter (8:1-3) with a preliminary shot across the bows of anyone who might suppose themselves so spiritually superior as to be above such discussions – we all have 'knowledge', do we? 'Knowledge' puffs you up; love builds you up. If anyone thinks they 'know' something, they don't yet know as they ought to know. But if anyone loves God – that person is known by God.

Shades of Galatians 4:8-11. Those who have believed the gospel of Jesus have come not just into a new 'knowledge' of God, but within the saving scope of the love of God. True monotheism isn't an opinion, a logical deduction, about God; it is being 'known' by the God who says to his people, Israel: You shall love the Lord your God with all your heart...

This combination of monotheistic affirmation and the command to love God takes us back to the very heart of Judaism, to the prayer, amounting to a confession of faith, said three times a day by devout Jews from Paul's time right up to the present. 'Hear, O Israel: the Lord our God, the Lord is One; and you shall love the Lord your God...' This is known as the *Shema*, from the Hebrew word for 'Hear' with which it opens. As so often in Paul, the text he alludes to one minute is the text he will then develop the next minute. Watch how he advances his argument.

Having cleared the ground in verses 1-3, he begins the real thrust of the chapter with as clear a statement of Jewish monotheism as one could wish to see. We know, he says, that no idol has any real existence (Galatians 4:8-11 again), and that there is no God but one. That is Jewish-style monotheism, ranged classically against pagan polytheism. Then, in typically Pauline style, never content to say a good thing once if he can expand it a bit, he continues by referring directly to, indeed quoting, the basic Jewish confession of faith, the *Shema*. In contrast, he says, to the many 'gods' and 'lords' of the pagan world, for us, he says, 'there is one God – the Father, from who are all things and we unto him – and one Lord – Jesus Christ, through whom are all things and we through him'. To feel the full force of this, we need to set it out side by side with the text Paul has in mind:

The Lord our God	One God – the Father...
The Lord is One	One Lord – Jesus Christ...
(Deuteronomy 6:4)	(1 Corinthians 8:6)

Faced with that astonishing statement, one would have to say that if the early Fathers of the church hadn't existed it would be necessary to invent them. Paul has redefined the very meaning of the words that Jews used, every day in their regular prayers, to denote the one true God. The whole argument of the chapter hinges precisely on his being a Jewish-style monotheist, over against pagan polytheism; and, as the lynchpin of the argument, he has quoted the most central and holy confession of that monotheism *and has placed Jesus firmly in the middle of it*. Lots of Pauline scholars have tried to edge their way round this one, but it can't be done. The nettle must be grasped. Somehow, Paul believes, the one and only God is now known in terms, at least, of 'father' and 'lord'. All things are made by the one; all things are made through the other.

This verse is one of the most genuinely revolutionary bits of theology ever written. It would be fair, though, to point out that Paul is standing on the shoulders of one of the traditions I mentioned a moment ago. According to some traditions, God's 'wisdom' is the one through whom the world was made. Similarly, in the passages where Paul speaks of God 'sending' his Son (Galatians 4:4; Romans 8:3-4), this too is the language of wisdom, sent by and from the creator to dwell among humans, specifically among Israel.

When I said Paul was standing on the shoulders of the Jewish Wisdom-tradition, I meant it. He can see a lot further than that tradition can; some Wisdom writers might be a bit uncomfortable supporting his weight. But what Paul glimpses from this new height is not just a bit of speculative fantasy. He has spied a new meaning of the word 'God', because the person he has firmly in view is Jesus of Nazareth, the crucified and risen one. Paul has taken the word 'God' itself and has filled it with new content. Or rather, he would say, he has discovered what its true content always was. What he knows to be true about Jesus leaves him no choice.

The same is true in the second passage, Philippians 2:5-11.

5 Have this mind among yourselves, which you have in Christ Jesus:
6 Who, though he was in the form of God,
Did not regard his equality with God as something to take advantage of,
7 But emptied himself, taking the form of a servant,
Being born in human likeness.
8 And, being found in human form, he humbled himself,
And became obedient to death, even the death of the cross.
9 Therefore God highly exalted him,
And freely gave him the name above all names,
10 That at the name of Jesus every knee should bow,
In heaven and on earth and under the earth,
11 And every tongue confess 'Jesus Christ is Lord!'
– To the glory of God the Father.

This is of course one of the most notoriously complex passages in all of Paul. We have already looked at one aspect of it. The further point I wish to make here can be spelt out fairly simply.

We begin at the end of the passage. There Paul declares (verses 10-11) that 'at the name of Jesus every knee shall bow... and every tongue confess that Jesus Christ is Lord, to the glory of God the Father.' Here, as in 1 Corinthians 8:6, Paul is quoting a monotheistic text from the Old Testament. Not just any miscellaneous monotheistic text, either. This comes from Isaiah 40–55, where we find the clearest and most sustained scriptural exposition and exaltation of the one true God over all false claimants, and at the same time the stoutest declaration of the sovereignty of the one God, ruling out all possibility of ontological dualism. Isaiah 45:23 declares, in the name of YHWH, Israel's one God: 'To me, and me alone, every knee shall bow, every tongue swear.' The whole point of the context is that the one true God does not, cannot and will not share his glory with anyone else. It is his alone. Paul, however, declares that this one God has shared his glory with – Jesus. How can this be? What on earth is he talking about?

The answer is found, of course, in the first half of the poem, if poem it be (2:5-8). Once we sort out some tricky technical language, what Paul is saying is this.

(1) Jesus was truly in the form of God, that is, he was equal with God. But (2) he did not regard this divine equality as something to exploit (watch out for different translations that get this vital point wrong). Instead, Paul says, (3) he offered the true interpretation of what it meant to be equal with God: he became human, and died under the weight of the sin of the world, obedient to the divine saving plan.

Why then has he been exalted, and given the name LORD? Because, quite simply, he has done what only the one true God can do. The truth about God is revealed, for Paul, supremely on the cross. As he says in Romans, 'God commends his love for us, in that while we were yet sinners Christ died for us.' That sentence, we should note, only makes sense if, somehow, God is fully and personally involved in the death of Jesus Christ. Paul's speculations (if we are right to call them that) about Jesus and God did not lead him into ever more complex flights of metaphysical fancy. They brought him face to face with the deep, utterly self-giving, utterly trustworthy, love of the covenant God, the God of Abraham, Isaac and Jacob.

Part of the point of Philippians 2, indeed, is a point not so much about Jesus as about God himself. The cross is not something that God does unwillingly or only because he can't think of a better way. At the heart of Philippians 2, and at the heart of Paul's theology and indeed gospel, is the news that the one true God consists, through and through, of self-giving love. For this God to become human, and to die for sinners, is not a category mistake, something that a sensible or logical God wouldn't do. At the climax of Isaiah 40–55 is a strange portrait of the servant of YHWH, who does for Israel and the world what only YHWH himself can do for the world. Yes, says Paul: Christ became a servant, and is now exalted in the glory which the one God will not share with one other than himself. Of course it will strain all our categories to breaking point and beyond. But if we are going to let Paul speak in his own terms we cannot help it. For him, the meaning of the word 'God' includes not only Jesus, but, specifically, the crucified Jesus. And it is this new meaning of the word 'God' that places Paul, as we saw in the previous chapter, into the thick of the battle between the true God and the rival gods: specifically, between the God of Israel, now revealed in Jesus of Nazareth, and the 'principalities and powers'; and, in particular, the pagan imperial claims of Caesar.

The third passage is Colossians 1:15-20.

> [15] He is the image of God, the invisible one
> firstborn of all creation
> [16] for in him everything was created
> in the heavens and on the earth
> the visible and the invisible
> whether thrones or dominions
> whether rulers or authorities
> everything has been created
> through him and for him.
>
> [17] And he is before all things
> and all things hold together in him;
> [18] And he is the head
> of the body, the church.
>
> He is the beginning
> the firstborn from the dead,
> so that in everything he might become pre-eminent
> [19] for in him all God's fulness
> was pleased to dwell

20 and through him to reconcile
everything to himself,
making peace by the blood of his cross,
whether things on the earth or things in the heavens.

This time the argument hinges on the parallelism between the two halves of the poem (1:15-18a; 1:18b-20). The poem is a classic example of Jewish monotheistic poetry, such as we find again and again in the psalms. The Jews, faced with the might and corruption of paganism, stressed repeatedly that the creator of the world was Israel's redeemer-God, and vice versa. If the creator were not their God, they would only have a local or tribal god, who could not be trusted to be stronger than anyone else's local or tribal god. By identifying YHWH as both the creator of the cosmos and the redeemer of Israel they safeguarded all their three basic doctrines: monotheism, election and eschatology. One God, one people of God, one future for Israel and the whole world.

And Paul has now written a poem in exactly this vein; but the central character is not YHWH, but Jesus. Or rather, as I think we must say, the central character is YHWH *now recognized* in the human face of Jesus. And once again the language is vaguely familiar. Once again Paul is standing on the shoulders of the writers who envisaged 'wisdom' as the means through which God made the world. Paul has gone beyond Jewish speculation, but he is not speculating. He is drawing conclusions from the death and resurrection of the Messiah.

These three central passages are of vital importance. They give the lie both to the suggestion that Paul did not, after all, identify Jesus very closely with the one God of Jewish monotheism, and to the opposite suggestion, that Paul was a Hellenist who, in divinizing Jesus, broke completely away from Jewish monotheism and invented, in effect, a new form of paganism. Neither of these will do.

These three passages do not stand alone. Once we have grasped the point which is, I think, seen clearest in them, dozens of other pieces of data cry out to be mentioned. In particular, we might note Paul's use of the phrase 'Son of God'. In Judaism, this usually refers either to Israel or, more specifically, to the king. It in no way suggests that the person concerned is part of the very being of God himself. For Paul, too, it remains true that the phrase still carries overtones of royal messiahship, and of Israel's identity as YHWH's true Son. But, equally, there should be no doubt that he has rethought the phrase, so that now, when he uses it, it means far more than previous Jews had meant by it. When he speaks of God 'sending his Son', in Galatians 4 and Romans 8; when he combines 'father' and 'son' in formulae, and indeed when he speaks of God as 'father' in close conjunction with a mention of Jesus Christ – then it appears that, for him, 'Son of God' has become a technical term with a new meaning. If we allow Paul to use his terms in his own way, I believe we are forced to conclude that the phrase meant *both* the Messiah, in whom Israel's destiny is summed up *and* the one who is sent, like Wisdom, from the creator, to accomplish his saving purposes. Paul discovered that in the language of messiahship there lay a hidden, hitherto unexploited potential. There is no tension, for him, between Jesus being the totally human Messiah, the representative of Israel, and the one who is sent as it were from God's side, to do and be what only God can do and be. Paul, in short, seems to have held what generations of exegetes have imagined to be an impossibility; a thoroughly incarnational theology, grounded in a thoroughly Jewish worldview.

The same point can be made through the word *Kyrios* or 'Lord'. I emphasized in the previous chapter that calling Jesus *Kyrios* flew directly in the face of the claims of Caesar. It is also clear, from a good many of the passages where Paul uses this word of Jesus (including, of course, two of those we have just examined), that it is for him a way of aligning Jesus personally, one-on-one, with the word *Kyrios* in the Septuagint (the Greek translation of the Hebrew Bible), where it regularly stands for YHWH, the not-to-be-pronounced Name of God. 'All who call upon the name of the Lord will be saved'. That verse (Romans 10:13) refers clearly to calling on the name of Jesus, to confessing Jesus specifically as *Kyrios* (10:9) and believing that God raised him from the dead. Yet the verse is a direct quotation from the prophet Joel (2:32, or 3:5 in the Greek version), where the natural assumption is that 'the Lord', *Kyrios*, is YHWH himself. Paul is not stupid. Again and again he is making the point, cryptically, which emerges into the light in the three passages we have examined more extensively, and in such startling throwaway lines as Romans 9:5, which introduces and prefigures precisely the point of 10:9-13: from the Jewish race comes the Messiah according to the flesh – who is also God over all, blessed for ever. (The attempts of worried scholars to find alternative ways of understanding this verse remain profoundly unconvincing.)

It was Paul's belief and contention, then, that at the heart of Jewish monotheism – within the oneness of the one God – lay a plurality, a reciprocal relationship. This, of course, strained at the borders of human language, even the God-given language of scripture; but one could clearly recognize 'the glory of God in the face of Jesus Christ' (2 Corinthians 4:6).

Paul, then, remained a monotheist of the Jewish variety. He continued to denounce pagan idolatry as blasphemous nonsense. He continued to regard pagan behaviour as immoral and dehumanizing. He continued to resist the blandishments of a dualism that would suggest that certain parts of creation (certain types of food and drink, for instance, or certain activities such as sex) were evil in and of themselves. Everything, he insisted, was God-given and good, and to be enjoyed when used in the proper way and the appropriate context (Romans 14:24, 20). He remained, in other words, at the centre of the map of Jewish monotheism. But, inside that monotheism itself, he had discovered Jesus: the crucified, risen and enthroned Jesus, the Lord of the world. And, intending to remain the most loyal of Jews, worshipping the one God of Abraham, Isaac and Jacob, he worshipped this Jesus.

Paul saw the human Jesus as the revelation of the one God. It mattered to him that this human being Jesus *remained* human, now that he was enthroned as the Lord of the world. But Jewish monotheism spoke of the one God dwelling with his people, animating, sustaining them, giving them life and hope. Theological reasons, as well as deep personal experience, therefore drove Paul to develop a further discovery at the heart of Jewish monotheism: the Spirit of God, also recognized as the Spirit of Jesus.

The Spirit Within Paul's Jewish Monotheism

There are once more three particular passages in which this point emerges clearly. If there was more space, literally dozens of others could then be drawn in to the argument.

To begin with, there is our old friend Galatians 4:1-7 (see above, page 58). Paul is here telling the story of Israel in slavery, and of how she attains her freedom. The background model for this is the exodus, the time when YHWH revealed himself in a new way to Israel. The foreground is the return from exile, when Israel, after her Babylonian and other bondage, is finally rescued, again in a great revelation of YHWH's sovereign and saving power. In both cases, this revelation of YHWH functions as a demonstration of the inadequacy and shabbiness of the pagan gods, Egyptian in the one case and Babylonian in the other.

Paul, in telling the story of how this redemption has actually been achieved, awakens echoes of both stories. He is clearly retelling the story of how the one true God has rescued a people for himself. But, as he tells it, the story comes out this time in a threefold form. The one true God sent his Son; then he sent the Spirit of his Son. The result (verses 8-11) is that these redeemed people now truly know the true God, or rather have been known by him; in other words, this Father-Son-Spirit combination is the true revelation of who the one true God is, which puts all other claimants to deity in the shade. Here, of course, Paul is able to draw not only on the Jewish language of wisdom, the one who is sent from the creator, but also on the language of Spirit itself, from various Jewish writings beginning with Genesis (1:2). The Spirit is not a being other than the one true God; to speak of God acting through his Spirit is to speak of God himself acting.

The second passage in which the key idea of 'God' is redefined in relation to the Spirit is 1 Corinthians 12:4-6. Here the context is very different, but the message is the same. Paul wants to stress to the Corinthians that, despite the diversity of functions and gifts in the church, there is only one God. Unity is his theme, and he stresses it throughout the chapter. But when he actually introduces the theme, it is a threefold unity of which he speaks:

> There are varieties of gifts, but the same Spirit;
> varieties of ministry, but the same Lord;
> varieties of working, but it is the same God working all in all.

Within the very stress on unity, Paul manages to suggest that this unity subsists in threefold form, and that these three are Spirit, Lord and God. But we should not make the mistake of thinking that Spirit and Lord are not, for him, also in some sense 'God', as we have already seen. He is at the borders of language, and his use of his own terms reflects the fact. The closer we get to his own terms, the more we discover that his view of God is (we have either to use the word or find a direct equivalent) trinitarian. It is emphatically not tritheist; there is only one God, as for Jewish monotheism. It is emphatically not pantheist; this God is not identified with the world. It is emphatically not Deist; this God is not distant or detached, but closely involved with the world. It is emphatically not modalist; the three are really distinct, since the middle term is the human being Jesus, who prayed to the

Father as Father, and who, for Paul, is no longer physically present in the same way as once he was. Paul does not solve the puzzle of how God can be three and one at the same time. But, for him, this is what the word God actually means. Even when he is using 'God' to denote the first member of the three, this member is now *defined in and by his intimate relation to* the other two. The creator is known as the Father of Jesus, as the sender of the Spirit.

The third and final passage about the Spirit introduces another major item into the discussion. In Romans 8:1-11, one of the great central passages for all of Pauline theology, we find Christ and the Spirit together doing what the Torah could not (verse 3). But we must remind ourselves that in Judaism, as indeed for Paul, Torah was not just a code of law. It was the living breath of the living God, identified by some writers with that Wisdom who was with the creator, acting as his agent, from the beginning of the world.

As the passage goes on, though, another aspect of this complex Jewish understanding of God-working-in-the-world becomes apparent. God sent his Son and his Spirit (like Wisdom in Ben-Sira 24) to do what Torah could not (Torah is identified with Wisdom in the same passage in Ben-Sira). The result is that the Spirit now *indwells* those who are in Christ (Romans 8:5-11). But this language of 'indwelling' comes directly from the third element in the same passage in Ben-Sira. There, Wisdom and Torah are identified with the Shekinah, the presence of the living God tabernacling in the Temple in Jerusalem, dwelling in the midst of his people. Paul is here ascribing to the Spirit that which was said of YHWH himself, living in the Temple. Paul has taken three of the ways in which good first-century Jewish monotheists conceived of the one true God acting within the world, and specifically within Israel; and he has used exactly these modes of speaking to describe what God has done in Jesus and the Spirit.

This is of course all the more startling when we consider Paul's view of the Christian and/or the church, who turn out, here as elsewhere in Paul, to be the new Temple. But for the moment we must notice that the passage forbids us to say anything less of the Spirit than that the Spirit, too, like the Son, belongs within the radically revised Jewish picture of the one true God. When Paul wants to speak of the ways in which the Son and the Spirit are related to the transcendent God who is beyond space and time, he uses exactly those language systems which some parts of Judaism had developed for speaking, within monotheism, of the ways in which this one God acted within the world. Paul remains completely a Jewish-style monotheist; but the one God is now known as God, Lord and Spirit; or Father, Lord, and Spirit; or God, Son, and Spirit; or various other combinations. For Paul, the very meaning of 'God' itself has been unpacked by and redefined in relation to the events and, if you like, the persons, of Jesus and the Spirit.

Paul, Jesus and God

It should be clear by now that when Paul went out into the Gentile world with his 'gospel', he went as a Jew to Gentiles, to tell the Gentile world what Jews had always believed: that 'the gods of the nations are idols, but our God made the heavens' (Psalm 96:5). But he had now been grasped by a new vision of God, which meant that the traditional statement could never be made casually or dismissively, with a sense of effortless racial superiority. The one God, the creator, had now been made known in and as Jesus of Nazareth, the crucified and risen Messiah, the Lord of the world. The face that called the world into existence was turned at last towards the world in self-revelation, in rescue, in love. The wind that swept over the waters of creation was blowing again, to bring to life things that were dead, to call into existence things that did not exist. This was a message, a thoroughly Jewish message, that the Gentile world urgently needed to hear. Paul believed himself called to be the means of bringing this about.

Ch. 1-4   Paul's orientation is thoroughly Jewish
He sees Jesus and the gospel as the
genuine fulfillment of Jewish O.T. faith
and hope.

CHAPTER 5

Good News
for the Pagans

As I look along my shelf of recent books on Paul, the titles reveal how the subject has been developing in the last twenty years. 'Paul and the law', or some variation thereon, accounts for half a dozen. 'Paul and Judaism', looking more widely, covers several others, notably W.D. Davies' *Paul and Rabbinic Judaism* and E.P. Sanders' *Paul and Palestinian Judaism*. Reading between the lines of some other titles, we find the same story: *Israel's Law and the Church's Faith* (S. Westerholm); *From Adam to Christ* (M.D. Hooker); even *The Mysticism of Paul the Apostle*, an older but evergreen work by Albert Schweitzer; these and many others speak of the interaction between Paul and his Jewish context. Those who have tried to go on explaining Paul as basically a Hellenist or Hellenizer have clearly been swimming against quite a strong tide. And even those who have tried to put Paul into his Hellenistic context in a more nuanced fashion, such as Wayne Meeks with his *First Urban Christians*, or Hans-Dieter Betz with his rhetorical analysis of Galatians, have refused to go all the way and say that Paul *derived* his central concepts from the pagan world.

I have no wish simply to swing the pendulum back again. As I have made clear in various writings, I regard the arguments in favour of a Jewish matrix for Paul's thought, and against a substantially Hellenistic one, as overwhelming, however many debates still obviously remain as to how we understand that Jewish matrix, and how, precisely, we fit Paul into it. Indeed, my argument in this chapter will in some ways reinforce this conclusion, albeit by a roundabout route. But at the same time I suspect that the discipline of Pauline studies as a whole, including paradoxically Meeks, Betz and others, has failed in recent years to take Paul's non-Jewish context as seriously as it might have done.

Paul, after all, describes himself, almost by definition, as the apostle to the *Gentiles* (Romans 1:5; 11:13; 15:16; Galatians 2:7-10; Ephesians 3:5-8). He has, as it appears from Romans 11 and elsewhere, a message for Jews as well (compare 1 Corinthians 9:20: 'to the Jews I became as a Jew, to win Jews'); but this is simply the reflex of his message to the Gentiles, not his main aim. Whatever we say about the picture in Acts, in which Paul tends to begin with the synagogue and then, when thrown out, turn to the local non-Jewish population, Acts itself clearly also supports the idea of Paul making a direct appeal to local Gentiles.

If this is anywhere near the mark, a whole set of questions emerges. These questions are not, indeed, unknown or unexamined, but they have been left to one side in much contemporary scholarship. I therefore have a proposal, and some specific suggestions, which will address this problem. I want, in short, to bring back into the light, to join the topic of Paul and Judaism, the equally intriguing one of Paul and paganism.

To begin with, a word about a word. We have learnt that there is no such thing as 'first-century Judaism', only first-century Judaisms, plural; the same is of course true in the non-Jewish world. What, after all, has Cicero in common with the worshippers of Diana at Ephesus, or Juvenal with either? The word 'pagan' is a convenient early Christian label to cover, as they might have said, a multitude of sins, much as the Jewish word 'Gentile' had done. Originally 'pagan' meant either a civilian (as opposed to a soldier) or a rustic (as opposed to a city-dweller). The former is the more likely derivation for the developed Christian meaning.

A more serious problem with the word is that it is inescapably loaded and biased. Worse: in the late twentieth century, as indeed in the time of the emperor Julian (AD332–63), it is loaded *both ways*. In our contemporary society there are some (in New Age circles, for instance) who use it as a praise-word, while several still regard it as a term of abuse. This makes it difficult to use in historical scholarship; but perhaps no more difficult than any of the alternatives. I am content to use the word 'pagan' in the broad sense in which classical scholars such as E.R. Dodds and Robin Lane Fox have used it – both of them, be it noted, scholars with more time and sympathy for the pagans than for the Christians. It is, like most such nouns, a large term to evoke a wide range of phenomena. It denotes, basically, those who are neither Jews nor Christians, and carries the connotation of their developed worldview, in which religion and politics, superstition and magic, hope and fear, and sometimes ethics and morals, cluster together around a bewildering range of symbols and stories, developed over many centuries and involving many quite diverse cultures.

Derivation and Confrontation

When people have studied Paul within his pagan context, they have usually been looking for the derivation of his key ideas. This, as I have indicated, is largely out of fashion in scholarly circles, though this has not prevented one recent popular writer[1] from suggesting that Paul's interpretation of the death of Jesus derived from the cult of Mithras, in which devotees stood underneath a platform and were drenched with the blood of a bull being sacrificed above (see chapter 10, below). But not only is this approach widely discredited among serious scholars; Paul himself would tell us that the question of 'derivation' was itself not the most important one to ask. In the study of Paul it is even more important to establish where his thought is going than to assess where it has come from. *Direction* is more important than *derivation*; *confrontation* is as important, if not more important than *conception*. That constitutes my proposal at the level of method.

At the level of content, my proposal is this. The direction of Paul's message was confrontation with paganism; he had good news for them, but it was good news which undermined their worldview and replaced it with an essentially Jewish one, reworked around Jesus. Since Paul saw himself as the apostle to the Gentiles, to the pagans, it is vital that we enquire how he conceived his message impinging on their consciousness, on their worldview, on what Lane Fox calls their 'religiousness' in a broad sense, not confined merely to cultic practices or theoretical beliefs, but involving deeply held attitudes which informed personal and corporate belief and behaviour at every point.

None of Paul's letters, of course, is addressed to a non-Christian pagan audience. The recipients are all Christians. Usually, they are Pauline Christians, though of course Romans at least is an exception, since Paul has not visited the church (this goes for Colossians, too). True, the Corinthian letters may be seen as Paul's attempt to hold that church to the Pauline nature of its Christianity, and to pull it back from the brink of a sort of semi-paganism. But to recover a sense of Paul's message to his non-Jewish hearers, we have to extrapolate from the letters as we have them, back to a hypothetical entity which may be supposed to underlie them.

At once we should realize the familiarity of this task, and the importance of the proposal at the level of an overall understanding of Paul. Recent scholarly debates about the nature of Pauline theology have tried to come to terms with the fact that this is what we have to do if we are not to allow the letters to collapse into simply a list of different 'theologies'. This discussion, in my experience, often gets bogged down, partly because many Pauline scholars are not equipped philosophically to handle the necessary questions of method, and partly because the debate regularly gets stuck on traditional issues such as justification and the law, and, in current discussion, over such questions as whether Paul was or was not a 'covenantal theologian', an 'apocalyptic theologian', or some combination of the two. I suggest that, instead of looking for an *abstract theological framework* which we can hypothesize and into which we can fit, or from which we can 'derive', the various specifics of the different letters, we would do far better to go in search of *Paul's work among the pagans*, including, but going beyond, his preaching and teaching. This was the controlling and guiding aim of his life. It may perhaps be the keystone refused by the builders which will nevertheless hold the arch together. This proposal is, I submit, at least worth a try.

If direction, rather than simply derivation, is the primary goal, what we must then expect to find is confrontation, not simply variation. This is where the history-of-religions method, for all its great achievements, regularly lets us down. Many scholars, seeing that Paul is critical of Judaism, have assumed that he must therefore have a non-Jewish theology. Many others, seeing that his theology was thoroughly Jewish, have then found it puzzling to explain how he came to hold a critique of Judaism. What the history-of-religions method, with its lines of derivation, is bad at discovering is *polemical engagement* on the one hand and *critique from within* on the other. Both, I suggest, play vital roles in Paul's missionary proclamation. We need to say a word about each.

Polemical Engagement (contextualization)

By 'polemical engagement' I mean that Paul becomes, as he says, all things to all people (1 Corinthians 9:22). He does not shout his message across a yawning cultural gap. Whatever we think about the historicity of the Areopagus speech in Acts 17, that speech exemplifies the principle Paul himself enunciates in 2 Corinthians 10:5, that of 'taking every thought captive to obey Christ'. This line of thought has been explored often enough in terms of Paul picking up his opponents' slogans in order to do something new with them. What is not so often noted is precisely what it is that he does with them. He seems to have believed what he (or someone else) wrote in Colossians 1:17 – all things were created through Christ and for Christ. He need not be afraid, then, in taking over, and using, key concepts from opposing systems of thought.

This does not lessen his opposition to the system in question. It does not mean that he has compromised, that he has taken a step down the slippery slope towards syncretism. Opposition to the older history-of-religions work has often come from conservative scholars because, quite rightly, they have perceived that whatever faults Paul may have had, syncretism was not one of them. But Paul's theology of creation was sufficiently robust for this not to be a problem. He took the high ground: all truth was, for him, God's truth, and when he took on an idea from pagan culture he made sure it was well and truly baptized before it could join the family. He claimed the high ground of the creational monotheist, not the split-level world of the worried dualist. Confrontation does not simply mean head-to-head total disagreement.

Paul's confrontation with paganism was of course sharp. He did indeed believe, and say, that certain beliefs were untrue, that certain practices were dehumanizing and simply wrong, and that certain styles of community life were not how the creator God had intended people to function. But Paul was no dualist. As we shall see, at the heart of his polemical engagement with paganism was a radical and deep-rooted affirmation of the goodness of the created world, and, with that, of the possibility that pagans, and their ideas and beliefs, could be redeemed by the Christ through whom the world was made in the first place. Hence, good news for the pagans; not the sort of good news that told them they were more or less all right as they were, but the sort of good news which told them that, though they were at present going about things in a totally wrong way, the God who made them loved them and longed to remake them.

The underlying reason for Paul's polemical engagement with pagan culture is not, I suggest, far to seek. But it is so frequently ignored that I should like to stress it here as of first importance. It is found in the Jewish expectations about how the purposes of the one God would eventually include the whole world.

81

These expectations, traceable back to the great prophets, emphasized that when Israel was finally redeemed, the Gentiles would share in the blessing. When Zion was restored, the nations would flock in to hear the word of Israel's God. When the Temple was rebuilt, rivers of living water would flow out to make the salt sea fresh. Obviously not all Jews of Paul's day shared this expectation. Equally obviously, I submit, Paul grasped it firmly.

Once we appreciate this point, Paul's mission to Gentiles can be seen in its proper light. It was not, as is sometimes suggested, a displacement activity, resulting from his puzzlement over Jewish rejection of his gospel. It was not an attempt to bolster his own flagging psyche. It was not the result of his being secretly in love all along with a thoroughly Hellenized Judaism, so that the gospel message became merely a new means of working on an agenda he already possessed, of turning Judaism into something quite different. Nor was it an activity which was designed to *produce* the great eschatological event – as though the death and resurrection of Jesus were mere detached events without climactic significance. No: the mission to the Gentiles was the natural corollary of Paul's belief that in the events of Jesus' death and resurrection, and the coming of the Spirit, *the promises of Israel's restoration had in fact been fulfilled*, in however initially paradoxical a fashion. If these things had happened, the New Age had dawned, and it was time for the Gentiles to come in. The God of Israel had called Israel into being in order to save the world; that was the purpose of election in the first place. The death and resurrection of the Messiah were not odd new events, bolts from the blue; in retrospect, they were to be seen as the coping-stone of the divine plan, which was always for the real exodus, not only of Israel, but of the whole world.

Paul's central beliefs thus naturally generated a mission in which polemical engagement was of the essence. He did not have to make the Jewish message into an essentially Gentile message for it to be audible or comprehensible to his pagan hearers; this old assumption, which still dominates Pauline scholarship in some quarters, is thoroughly misleading and unhistorical. What the Gentiles needed was precisely the Jewish message, or rather the Jewish message *as fulfilled in Jesus the Messiah*. The whole older history-of-religions movement trembles at the thought of a *Jewish* message for a *pagan* world; yet that, for thoroughly comprehensible reasons, is what Paul offers.

The nature of this polemical engagement is thus that Paul is claiming the high ground from his pagan hearers. The Jewish message is precisely not that there is another god to choose from among so many, another set of religious practices to take their stand in the market-place. The Jewish message, as we shall presently see, focused of course on monotheism, and this monotheism was of a particular variety, namely creational and covenantal monotheism, as opposed to the pantheism of the Stoics, or the syncretistic monotheism achieved by lumping all or most of the pagan deities together, or the henotheism of those who worshipped one of the pagan deities and called them 'the one'. The Jewish belief in the creator meant that any Jew who cared to do so (and Paul certainly cared to do so) could address the pagan world with a message from its true God, its creator. The message, paradoxically, *had* to remain essentially Jewish if it was to have its proper relevance to the pagans. If it had been translated into pagan categories it would have competed with them for their own turf. It would have made YHWH one God among the other gods. By remaining what it was, it claimed the high ground of genuine creational monotheism.

Paul's polemical engagement with paganism, however, was not exactly like a non-Christian Jewish engagement might have been. It involved, as its reflex, a critique of Judaism. But it was not a critique from outside, from a pagan standpoint. It was a critique from within.

Critique from Within

Paul hints in various passages that his vocation was like that of a prophet (e.g. Galatians 1:15, echoing Isaiah 49:1 and Jeremiah 1:5). This hints at the nature of his critique of Judaism. The prophet does not criticize Israel from a non-Jewish standpoint; he claims to represent Israel's true vocation and belief, calling her back to an allegiance to her God from which she had declined. Though he may be regarded as a disloyal Jew, the prophet always claims the high ground: he stands for true loyalty, which the present regime or ideology is abandoning (compare Elijah's exchange with Ahab in 1 Kings 18:17-18). The prophet's task is to speak from the heart of the tradition, to criticize and warn those who, claiming to represent the tradition, are in fact abandoning it.

This is this task, I suggest, that Paul sees himself undertaking in such passages as Galatians 3–4, Philippians 3, and several sections of Romans. His critique of Israel should not be read as a denial of the doctrine of election, a rejection of the belief that the Jewish people were chosen by the one true God to be his means of saving the world. The critique is, rather, the cutting edge of that doctrine, seen from the point of view of the Jew who believes that the crucified and risen Jesus is the Messiah around whom Israel is now defined. Paul argues that ethnic Israel has failed in the purpose for which she was called into being. He does not suggest that God's choice of Israel was a bad thing, nor yet that God has changed his mind about it. His point is that Israel, the chosen people, has failed to accomplish the mission to which she was called. That is, Israel as a whole has failed; Israel's representative, the Messiah, Jesus, has succeeded. As we shall see, deep at the heart of what Paul believes about Jesus is that he was the true, representative Israelite.

So far, indeed, is Paul from standing in a pagan position from which to criticize his fellow Jews that he adopts instead the standpoint of the great proto-prophet, Moses, pleading with the covenant God for his errant people (Romans 9:1-5, 10:1-2; compare Exodus 32–33). The significance of this should not be missed. Moses pleaded with God for an Israel that was becoming pagan, worshipping the golden calf and behaving accordingly. Paul sees himself as doing the same.

Paul is again claiming the high ground. He expounds Genesis 15, and many other passages, to say that Israel's true fulfilment is now to be found in Jesus Christ and the Spirit. Israel rejected the call of Jesus, and now rejects the apostolic message *about* Jesus, because it challenges that which has become her all-consuming interest: her relentless pursuit of national, ethnic and territorial identity. She is, Paul reckons, in danger of making herself simply a nation 'like all the others'. Blood and soil were the marks of pagan nations; Israel was using Torah and circumcision to emphasize exactly those things. Thus her circumcision had become mere pagan-style mutilation (Philippians 3:2); her adherence to Torah had become mere pagan-style allegiance to principalities and powers (Galatians 4:8-11); and her whole system stood condemned as being now driven by the 'Adamic' nature that made Adam's trespass to abound in the very place (i.e. Israel) where Torah was given (Romans 5:20, 7:7-25). When Paul coins somewhat contemptuous puns to make this point (for instance, *katatome*, 'mutilation', for *peritome*, 'circumcision', in Philippians 3:2), this is not mere angry invective. It is the equivalent of what would happen today if a would-be loyal Jew, living in the land of Israel and yearning for a just peace with all her neighbours, were to look out on the work of right-wing activists and refer to them as the '*Un*settlers'. It is a way of pointing out that extreme zeal has a habit of achieving the opposite end from that which it is ostensibly seeking. It is a critique from within.

This leads us back, for a moment, to the zeal which characterized Saul of Tarsus before the Damascus Road event. Notice what has now happened. We saw in chapter 2 that Saul's zeal had two focal points. First, it meant relentless opposition to the paganism which surrounded and infiltrated his Jewish world. Second, it meant zealous promotion of Torah observance among his Jewish contemporaries, even to the extent of violence against those who were compromising. I have now suggested that Paul the Christian retained this dual focus, but with a radical change of emphasis in both. He still saw the message of the true God as challenging the false gods. He still saw the great mass of Judaism as being disloyal to the true God, and needing to be brought into line. But the line in question was now the Christian, the fulfilled-Israel, line. Paul's zeal to confront the pagans with the message of the true God, and his critique of his fellow Jews as the reflex of that confrontation, retain the shape of the zeal of Saul of Tarsus. But now the God for whom he is zealous is seen in a very different light. Now, he would say – I have a zeal for God, but it is according to knowledge; because in Christ I know God, or rather am known by him (comparing Romans 10:2 and 1 Corinthians 8:2-3).

This chapter so far has constituted a proposal for an approach to Paul which has not been much explored, though it has a good deal to commend it. We must now turn to some of the details. What precisely was the message which Paul had for the pagan world? How did it subvert the worldview of paganism itself?

The Challenge: Reality and Parody

We begin with a word of caution. People have often attempted to explain the rapid growth of Christianity by arguing that the first-century pagan world was, so to speak, 'ready for Christianity'. I am not so sure. The Athenians were not ready to hear about 'Jesus and resurrection' (Acts 17:18, 32). I don't think the Corinthians were particularly ready to be told about a new way of being human which involved chastity and the renunciation of party spirit. The Philippians, as we have already seen, will have been radically challenged by hearing that Jesus was the one true *Kyrios*, the lord of all the world. It may be true that people were tired of Stoicism, though Epictetus, Paul's near-contemporary, gives no sign of it. It may be true that people were tired of Epicureanism, though Paul addresses it as a live option in Athens. It may be true that people were fed up with the ordinary pagan cult, and indeed Pliny, writing in the early second century, suggests that it was honoured as much in the breach as in the observance in his day. But the basic features of paganism were deeply engrained in the lives and habits of ordinary people. Sacrifice, holy days, oracles, inspection of auspices, mystery-cults, and a good deal else besides were part of the daily world of Paul's audience. My sense is that the pagan world was no more 'ready for the gospel', in that sense, than the Jewish world was ready to hear the news of a crucified Messiah.

Paul's challenge to the pagan world was not, then, a matter of filling in a set of blanks in a system already conscious of them. It was a matter of announcing a truth which, from Paul's point of view, was the reality of which paganism was the parody. I suggest six areas in which this will have been the case; there may well be more. In each case what I have to say functions as an indication of a huge subject which could and should be developed much further.

God and creation

First, Paul offered the reality of the true God, and the creation as his handiwork. This Paul saw as the reality, over against the paganism which, though aware of the existence of the creator, constantly identified him with objects or forces within creation itself. It is remarkable how little attention has been given to Paul's view of God; where it has been studied, this has been mostly in relation to normal Jewish views. I suggest that Paul's zeal for the God he now saw revealed in the face of Jesus Christ gave him a well-worked out and freshly articulated version of the normal Jewish critique of pagan idolatry.

We see this, I think, underlying such passages as Colossians 1:15-20. Here we have the highest possible affirmation of the goodness, and God-givenness, of the created world, without the slightest danger of this affirmation leading to a pagan divinization of creation. In the middle of this, Paul was also offering a fuller and more complete account of who precisely the one creator God actually was. As I have argued elsewhere, he remains firmly within the boundaries of Jewish-style creational monotheism, while at the same time exploring and celebrating the inner being of the one God in terms of Creator, Lord and Spirit, or of Father, Lord and Spirit, or of Creator, Son and Spirit, or whatever. This is perhaps one of the most basic things that a pagan audience would have picked up: Paul stood over against the multiplicity of gods with the news of the one God, and stood over against the divinization of creation with the news of the createdness of creation – without any suggestion that creation was therefore less than good.

Cult and religion

Second, Paul was therefore offering a clear challenge at the level of cult. The pagan world was, one might almost say, infested with gods of every sort and for every purpose. Whatever one might undertake, from going through a door to undertaking a sea voyage, from getting married to planting a tree, there were gods to be placated and propitiated. Sacrifice was ubiquitous in the ancient world, producing often enough far more meat than could be eaten by those directly involved, which resulted in the problem we encountered in 1 Corinthians 8–10, of sacrificial meat being sold in the open market.

The interesting thing for our present purposes about Paul's answer to the problem is the way in which he appears almost to sail close to the wind. Part of his answer constitutes the first written theology of the Christian eucharist; and he argues from that to the incompatibility of sharing the table of the Lord and the table of demons. He addresses the problem not as an isolated 'moral issue', to be answered with a simple rule of thumb, but by thinking through what the Christian community actually is: the fulfilment of the community of Israel, with its symbols picking up the Jewish symbols, particularly those which evoked the exodus from Egypt (1 Corinthians 10). The eucharist is, for Paul, the feast which shows that the church is the true exodus community. But, precisely at the same time, the eucharist is the feast which challenges the tables of the demons as realities challenge parodies. When confronted with paganism, Pauline theology does not collapse into dualism, leaving paganism with the high ground of celebrating creation. Rather, Paul sees the crucifixion of Jesus, and the Christian celebration of that event, as being the final truth towards which paganism, seen with maximum generosity, could be said to be straining. Paul has not *derived* his view of the eucharist from the pagan mysteries or sacrificial cults. It grows directly from its Jewish roots. But, just for that reason, it offers itself as the reality of which pagan cults are the shadowy parody.

Power and empire

Third, Paul offered a clear challenge to paganism at the level of power, particularly of empire. If we begin by analyzing Paul's theology in terms simply of justification by faith, we will find, as many have done, that his language about the principalities and powers falls off the back. But if we begin by asking, as I have suggested we should, how his gospel confronted the pagan world, such issues become once again central and vital.

We have already seen how in Philippians 2 and 3 Paul explicitly (and we must assume deliberately) speaks of Jesus in language which echoes, and hence deeply subverts, language in common use among Roman imperial subjects to describe Caesar. In the pagan world of Paul's day, particularly in the Eastern empire but increasingly in Rome itself, it was natural for emperors to be treated with divine honour. Already in the time of Tiberius, his predecessor, Augustus, was regarded as divine, so that the emperor became first the son of a god and then, in turn, a god himself. *Kyrios Kaisar* was the formula which said it all: Caesar is Lord.

Most pagans within the Roman world were quite happy to acknowledge Caesar as Lord; they did it politically, and doing it religiously was all part of the same overarching package. And Paul said: no, *Kyrios Iesous Christos*: Jesus Christ is Lord. In particular, he said this when addressing a community for whom, based in a Roman colony, the lordship of Caesar was a very live issue. He must have known what he was doing. In addition to the wealth of Jewish theology which lies behind the Christology of Philippians, particularly chapter 2, there is a clear sense of confrontation with one of paganism's treasured heartlands, the imperial ideology. We know that, a hundred years after Paul, the aged bishop Polycarp was burnt at the stake for refusing to offer token worship to Caesar. He stands in a direct line of descent from Philippians 2.

Here again we note the difference between derivation and confrontation. The *derivation* of Paul's Christology in Philippians 2 is clearly Jewish. But precisely that Jewish matrix, particularly Isaiah 40–55, gives Paul the belief that when the true God becomes king, all the false gods find themselves dethroned. The Jewish derivation thus generates the *confrontation* with paganism. The powers of the world are confronted with the one who is the true Lord of all.

True humanness

Fourth, Paul set out *a way of being human* which undercut the ways of being human on offer within paganism. In what we call his ethical teaching, in his community development, and above all in his theology and practice of new life through dying and rising with Christ, he articulated, inculcated, and urged upon his converts a way of life which he saw as being the genuinely human way of life. He saw paganism as a self-destructive mode of being human. He offered instead a way of being human which, based firmly on its Jewish foundations, had been reworked in the light of Jesus and the Spirit. This way of life, he believed, would truly do what, prior to his conversion, he had always supposed the Torah would do, namely, take on paganism and beat it on its own ground. In his theology of community, he replaced the Roman empire (under the rule of the ironically styled 'prince of peace') with the *imperium* of Jesus Christ, the true Prince of Peace, whom to serve means living in love with all one's brothers and sisters. If Jesus (as I have argued elsewhere) offered his hearers a counter-Temple movement, Paul offered his a counter-empire movement. No wonder people thought him dangerous.

The true story of the world

Fifth, Paul was telling the true story of the world in opposition to pagan mythology. It is very ironic that, in the last century, a good deal of early Christianity has been analyzed in terms of myth-making. In fact, a fair amount of it, not only in Paul, intended to tell the story of what had actually happened within recent human history, and to show that these events were the real revelation of the one true God. A glance at any book on the myths of ancient paganism will show once more what is going on here. The Christian story, to be sure, *functions* as 'myth' in the sense that it is the story told by the community to explain and sustain its common life. But, unlike the myths of Greece and Rome, the story told by Paul and the others only made sense insofar as it was the true story, the story of things that actually happened in recent history in the real world. Paul was inviting his hearers to come to terms with reality: not just a 'spiritual' reality in the sense of an otherworldly, invisible reality, or a private 'spiritual' experience, but with the earthly reality, the flesh-and-blood reality, of Jesus of Nazareth and his death and resurrection. What is more, Paul offered his hearers a story in which the whole cosmos was *going somewhere*. Against the essentially ahistorical worldview of paganism, and over against the 'golden age' dreams of some philosophers of history, Paul articulated a linear view of history, from creation to new creation. This offered to the pagan world a historical map, with a sign (the resurrection and the Spirit) saying 'You Are Here'. Romans 8 makes this point (as it makes so many) remarkably clearly. Paul affirms the goodness of the created world, and locates himself and his hearers with the resurrection of Jesus behind them and the liberation of all creation ahead of them. The New Age has been inaugurated, and will one day be consummated.

We can see this to particular advantage if we consider Paul's basic *kerygma* (proclamation or announcement) in 1 Corinthians 15:3-8. Deciding it is about time to remind his Corinthian congregation of the terms in which he preached the gospel to them, and to expound it more fully, he goes, of course, for the central events: Christ died for our sins according to the scriptures, he was buried, he was raised on the third day according to the scriptures, and he was seen by Cephas, James, five hundred at once, and last of all by Paul himself. Already it should be clear that Paul's gospel to the pagans was not a philosophy of life. Nor was it, even, a doctrine about how to get saved. It was a list of facts; not uninterpreted facts, of course, since no such things exist, but a list of events set within a framework which makes their import clear. What has the pagan world to do with the strange events concerning Jesus of Nazareth? Answer: they are not simply odd Jewish occurrences, but are the fulfilment of the creator's plan for the whole cosmos. As becomes very clear in the ongoing argument, talk of Jesus and his resurrection is talk about the creator of the world – more specifically, talk about how the creator is, through Jesus, becoming the true king of all the world. The Jewish framework of interpretation within which Paul understands and expounds the death and resurrection of Jesus is, of course, apocalyptic: that is, these events carry cosmic significance. This is the good news for the pagans: that the creator of the world will be all in all, by defeating evil and death and claiming the world as his own.

Paul is, in other words, once more claiming the high ground. This is ironic, considering the way in which 'apocalyptic' has often been regarded as dualistic. The whole world belongs to the one true God, who is now reclaiming it. God is not simply affirming the world as it stands: that would be to capitulate to paganism, with its worship of all sorts of elements within the world as though they were themselves divine. It would be to ignore the fact of evil and corruption, decay, misery and death which now deface God's creation. Nor is Paul rejecting the world as it stands, as though the Christian gospel were a form of dualism. He is saying, as he says extensively in Romans 8, that the whole creation is longing for its exodus, and that when God is all in all even the division between heaven and earth, God's space and human space, will be done away with (as we see also in Revelation 21). Paul's message to the pagan world is the fulfilled-Israel message: the one creator God is, through the fulfilment of his covenant with Israel, reconciling the world to himself. This involves, it seems, a triple exodus. Israel is redeemed, in the person of Jesus, for the sake of the world. Humankind is redeemed, through Jesus, so that the image of God may be restored. Thus creation itself is redeemed, and the creator God will be all in all.

Philosophy and metaphysics

Sixth, Paul offered an implicit challenge to the major pagan philosophies of the Roman world. He says, after all, that he offers the true wisdom of the creator God, over against the spurious wisdom of the pagan philosophical world. Once again, he draws on his Jewish tradition, rethought in and through Jesus Christ and the Spirit, to confront paganism and beat it on its own ground.

In his famous book *On the Nature of the Gods*, Cicero outlines the three serious philosophical options open to a thinking person in the Greco-Roman world of the first century BC. You could be a Stoic: that is, you could be a monist or pantheist, believing that everything that exists is somehow either divine or impregnated with the divine. You could be an Epicurean: that is, you could believe that, though the gods may exist, they are a long way away from us, and do not concern themselves with our world. (The best thing you can then do is to order your life to give yourself the least trouble and most quiet contentment.) Or you could be, as Cicero was himself, an Academician, taking the sceptical view that we can't really know about these things too much anyway, and the best thing to do is simply to keep up the old pagan cultic practices, the sacrifices, the auguries and so forth (Cicero himself was, like many other highly placed Romans, a cult official), and hope that society somehow holds together around them. It didn't, of course, and Cicero was himself the victim of its disintegration. But what would Paul have said, had he read Cicero's book?

It's an interesting question — I don't know why there isn't a whole monograph on the subject. Basically, I think he would have said to Cicero himself, as a sceptical Academician, that he was right to be sceptical about the fantastic and often laughable claims that are regularly made for the gods of the pagan pantheon. One can't indeed know very much about them, because they either don't exist or are disguises for shadowy and demonic forces. But he would have insisted that one can indeed know for sure about the one true God, the God of Abraham, Isaac and Jacob; one can know about him, even beyond the borders of Israel, because he has revealed himself to all in raising Jesus from the dead, and in establishing through the Spirit of Jesus a family in which all humans are equally welcome, a family destined to inherit the world.

To the Stoic, Paul would have agreed that the world is indeed a place where God's power and beauty are seen. But he would have insisted that this is not because the world itself is in some sense divine, but because it is the good creation of the good and wise God – and because this God intends to flood all creation with his presence, so that the world, like a chalice, is beautiful not because of what it is but because of what it is designed to be filled with.

To the Epicurean, Paul would have agreed that the true God was indeed different from the world, not to be identified or confused with it. But he would have strongly denied that this true God was distant from, or unconcerned with, the world. Rather, in the history of Israel and supremely in Jesus Christ, he is passionately and compassionately involved with the world. The Sceptic, the Stoic and the Epicurean would thus be confronted with Paul's essentially Jewish theology, redrawn around Christ and the Spirit. It is an interesting reflection that what I have just described, more or less, is the address which Luke puts into Paul's mouth when he addressed the Elders of Athens (Acts 17:22-31).

Conclusion

We are now in a position to compare and contrast the agendas of Saul of Tarsus (chapter 2 above) with the agendas of Paul the apostle. My argument has been that the 'zeal' with which Saul of Tarsus went about his pre-Christian agendas was replaced, in Paul's vocation to be the apostle to the pagans, with a new sort of 'zeal', similar in shape but radically different in content.

Like Saul of Tarsus, Paul believed, first, that the God of Israel had a quarrel with paganism. But instead of wanting to defeat paganism with its own weapons, i.e. violence and racial prejudice, Paul the apostle believed it was his task to announce to the pagan world that the true God had revealed himself in his crucified and risen Son, thereby summoning the whole world to repentance (which meant, very concretely, turning from idols) and allegiance. He was offering the truly human way of life to people who, by their idolatry and immorality, were destroying their very humanity. Paul's zeal in the proclamation of the gospel to the pagans, and in the maintenance of churches on pagan soil, replaced the first basic thrust of the zeal of Saul of Tarsus.

Second, like Saul of Tarsus, Paul the apostle believed that the God of Israel also had a quarrel with those of Israel who were disloyal. Saul, however, wanted to root out such fellow-Jews as had failed to see the light by the means of violence and ever more stringent Torah reinforcement. Paul believed it was his task so to win over the Gentile world into the family of Abraham – so to graft unnatural branches into the natural olive tree – that the true family, the natural branches, would be made jealous and want to return to the privileges they had spurned when they rejected, and continued to reject, their God-sent Messiah (Romans 11).

Like Saul of Tarsus, therefore, Paul the apostle believed that the scriptural prophecies had been designed to come true in a great act which would reveal that the God of Israel was the one true God of all the world. This great event would show that Israel was God's people, and that the pagan world was in the wrong, and would bow the knee before the true God.

But, unlike Saul, Paul believed that the great act had already occurred. Instead of a great military victory over Rome, Jesus as the representative Israelite had won a great victory over sin and death, the real enemies of the people of God and of the whole world. This great act did indeed demonstrate that the God of Israel was the one true God. This great act did indeed tell the pagan world that it was wrong, and that it was time to bow the knee before the true God. But it did so in a way which left the Jew as humbled as the pagan before the revelation of God's grace.

Paul continued to believe, as Saul had done, that one could tell, in the present, who was a member of the true people of God. For Saul, the badge was Torah: those who kept Torah strictly in the present were marked out as the future true Israel. For Paul, however, that method would only intensify the great gulf between Jew and Gentile, which the death and resurrection of the Messiah had obliterated. Rather, now that the great act had already occurred, the way you could tell in the present who belonged to the true people of God was quite simply faith: faith in the God who sent his Son to die and rise again for the sake of the whole world. This is the point at which, as we shall see in the next two chapters, the doctrine of 'justification by faith' becomes crucially relevant in Paul's mission to the pagan world. It was not the message he would announce on the street to the puzzled pagans of (say) Corinth; it was not the main thrust of his evangelistic message. It was the thing his converts most needed to know in order to be assured that they really were part of God's people.

I believe, as a historian, theologian and exegete, that the task which I have just begun in this chapter, of analyzing Paul's message to the pagan world, is an essential one if we are to understand him and his theology in their proper perspective. This is the line he himself suggests to us, and it is absurd that scholarship should rumble on without addressing it fully. There is, however, another dimension to this task. I believe, as a matter of cultural analysis, that the Western world is moving rapidly towards various new forms of paganism. I have offered a brief analysis of this in my book *New Tasks for a Renewed Church* (published in America as *Bringing the Church to the World*). The church, ironically enough, has often majored on the message that Paul had, not to the pagans, but to the world of Judaism. That remains important. But we do not have to tell our hearers to become Jews in order that they may then be confronted by Paul's gospel. If we want to address our own generation with the message of Jesus Christ, we need to rediscover the way in which that gospel really is good news for a pagan world. Paul is very zealous about that, if only we will listen to him.

But if Paul had good news for the pagans, what did he have to say to his fellow Jews? We have glanced at his critique of them: he warned them against what he saw as the paganization of their own tradition. But did he not have good news for them as well?

Notes

1. A.N. Wilson, *Paul: The Mind of the Apostle*, 1997, page 71.

CHAPTER 6

Good News for Israel

We have just seen that Paul's basic vocation was to be the apostle to the Gentiles, the pagans. But the whole point of this vocation was that what the pagans needed to hear was the good news of the God of Israel, the creator of the world. The Gentiles would be blessed, according to the particular Jewish hope that Paul seems to have cherished, when and only when Israel's God fulfilled his promises to, and purposes for, Israel. Paul believed that this had already happened – in Jesus, the Jewish Messiah, and his death and resurrection. How could this be? How could these extraordinary events be the unveiling of covenant plan of Israel's God? And what would this all mean for Israel?

We also saw, in chapter 4, that Paul had taken the central Jewish picture of God and had, from within the possibilities latent in that Jewish picture, redrawn it around Jesus and the Spirit. We shall now see that he did exactly the same with the central Jewish belief about what this God was supposed to be doing, or to be about to do, within the history of Israel and the world. This leads us to the heart of what was arguably Paul's greatest letter. It also introduces us to one of his most crucial and controversial technical terms: the phrase *dikaiosune theou*, whose least inadequate translation is perhaps 'the righteousness of God'.

One initial note about language. English speakers need to bear in mind, throughout this and the following chapter, that there are two quite different English roots which regularly translate the same Greek root. *Dikaios* means 'righteous', but also 'just'. *Dikaiosune* means 'righteousness', but also 'justice'. Unfortunately, when we come to the cognate verb, *dikaioun*, we can say 'to justify', but we cannot, in normal English usage, say 'to righteous'. (E.P. Sanders has tried this, but the habit has not caught on; an older English form, 'to rightwise', was used in the translation of Bultmann's *New Testament Theology*, but this, too, has not been taken up subsequently.) This would not matter so much if we could always say 'just' and 'justice' instead of 'righteous' and 'righteousness'. But, though the latter pair are themselves misleading in their current English meaning, the former would be even more so. The problem – typical of many that meet the reader of Paul at every turn – is of course that Paul is writing in Greek, but aware of the Hebrew scriptures that stand behind what he wants to say; and that we are writing in English, vainly attempting to find words and phrases which catch the flavour and emphasis of what was already a subtle and intricate train of thought. It is like translating poetry. Maybe that is actually what we are trying to do.

Covenant, Law court and Eschatology

'The righteousness of God' has been the subject of many major and technical studies. I shall not pretend here, any more than elsewhere in this book, that I have given you the full story on every aspect of it. The term, or something so close as to be clearly identical, occurs eight times in Paul, seven of which are in Romans. Its meaning is quite drastically obscured in various translations, not least in the crucial passage Romans 3:21-26; the New International Version, for instance, has Paul meaning at least two quite different things by the phrase within the space of these six verses. What I shall do is to sketch out the Jewish context within which the phrase would naturally be heard, indicate the options that different schools of thought have suggested for its interpretation, and argue for what seems to me to be the right solution.

For a reader of the Septuagint, the Greek version of the Jewish scriptures, 'the righteousness of God' would have one obvious meaning: God's own faithfulness to his promises, to the covenant. God's 'righteousness', especially in Isaiah 40–55, is that aspect of God's character because of which he saves Israel, despite Israel's perversity and lostness. God has made promises; Israel can trust those promises. God's righteousness is thus cognate with his trustworthiness on the one hand, and Israel's salvation on the other. And at the heart of that picture in Isaiah there stands, of course, the strange figure of the suffering servant through whom God's righteous purpose is finally accomplished.

There are many other passages which support this reading of 'God's righteousness'; for instance, the great prayer of Daniel 9. But the point is not controversial. In the Septuagint, the phrase means, most naturally, God's faithfulness to his covenant with Israel, as a result of which he saves her from her exile in Babylon. There are a good many occurrences of the phrase, or close cognates, in second-temple Jewish literature; they all reinforce this basic reading. At the heart of 'God's righteousness' is his covenant with Israel, the covenant through which he will address and solve the problem of evil in and for the whole world.

Part of the particular flavour of the term, however, comes from the metaphor which it contains. 'Righteousness' is a forensic term, that is, taken from the law court. This needs to be unpacked just a bit.

The Hebrew law court

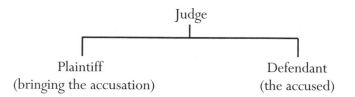

1. In the (biblical) Jewish law court there are three parties: the judge, the plaintiff and the defendant. There is no 'director of public prosecutions'; all cases take the form of one party versus the other party, with the judge deciding the issue.

2. What does it mean to use the language of 'righteousness' in this context? It means something quite different when applied to the judge to what it means when applied to either the plaintiff or the defendant. Applied to the judge, it means (as is clear from the Old Testament) that the judge must try the case according to the law; that he must be impartial; that he must punish sin as it deserves; and that he must support and uphold those who are defenceless and who have no-one but him to plead their cause. For the judge to be 'righteous', to have and practise 'righteousness' in this forensic setting, is therefore a complex matter to do with the way he handles the case.

3. For the plaintiff and the defendant, however, to be 'righteous' has none of these connotations. They, after all, are not trying the case. Nor, less obviously to us because of the moral overtones the word 'righteous' now has in our own language, does the word mean that they are, before the case

starts, morally upright and so deserving to have the verdict go their way. No; for the plaintiff or defendant to be 'righteous' in the biblical sense *within the law-court setting* is for them to have that status *as a result of the decision of the court.*

How does this work out? Let us take the plaintiff first. If and when the court upholds the plaintiff's accusation, he or she is 'righteous'. This doesn't necessarily mean that he or she is good, morally upright or virtuous; it simply means that in this case the court has vindicated him or her in the charge they have brought.

It is the same with the defendant. If and when the court upholds the defendant, acquitting him or her of the charge, he or she is 'righteous'. This, again, doesn't necessarily mean that he or she is good, morally upright or virtuous; simply that he or she has, in this case, been vindicated against the accuser; in other words, acquitted.

Of course, the word *dikaios*, 'righteous', in secular Greek as in English, carried moralistic overtones. Granted this, it is not hard to see how it could come to refer not just to a status held after the decision of the court, but also to the character and past behaviour of either the plaintiff or the defendant. But the key point is that, within the technical language of the law court, 'righteous' means, for these two persons, *the status they have when the court finds in their favour.* Nothing more, nothing less.

The result of all this should be obvious, but is enormously important for understanding Paul. If we use the language of the law court, it makes no sense whatever to say that the judge imputes, imparts, bequeaths, conveys or otherwise transfers his righteousness to either the plaintiff or the defendant. Righteousness is not an object, a substance or a gas which can be passed across the courtroom. For the judge to be righteous does not mean that the court has found in his favour. For the plaintiff or defendant to be righteous does not mean that he or she has tried the case properly or impartially. To imagine the defendant somehow receiving the judge's righteousness is simply a category mistake. That is not how the language works.

What happens, then, when we put the covenantal meaning of God's righteousness together with the metaphorical level drawn from the law-court scene? God, of course, is the judge. Israel comes before him to plead her case against the wicked pagans who are oppressing her. She longs for her case to come to court, for God to hear it, and, in his own righteousness, to deliver her from her enemies. She longs, that is, to be justified, acquitted, vindicated. And, because the God who is the judge is also her covenant God, she pleads with him: be faithful to your covenant! Vindicate me in your righteousness!

'Enter not into judgment with your servant, O Lord, for in your sight shall no man living be justified!' Psalm 143, in fact, from which those words come, forms a typical statement of the Jewish hope: covenantal, shot through with metaphorical law-court overtones. It also happens to be the psalm Paul quotes at a crucial turn in his argument (Romans 3:20).

If and when God does act to vindicate his people, his people will then, metaphorically speaking, have the status of 'righteousness'. I shall have a good deal more to say about this in the next chapter, when we look at the cognate topic of justification. *But the righteousness they have will not be God's own righteousness.* That makes no sense at all. God's own righteousness is his covenant faithfulness, because of which he will (Israel hopes) vindicate her, and bestow upon her the status of 'righteous', as the vindicated or acquitted defendant. But God's righteousness remains, so to speak, God's own property. It is the reason for his acting to vindicate his people. It is not the status he bestows upon them in so doing.

In all this discussion it is clear that we must add one further dimension to the discussion. If the covenant between God and Israel is the basic context of meaning within which righteousness-language finds its home; and if the law court is the metaphorical context which gives particular colour to that covenantal language; then both contexts demand that there be a future fulfilment. Eschatology – the long hope of Israel for her God to act at last, once and for all – must be brought in at every point.

But what is this hope? God's righteousness is what Israel invokes when she is in trouble, in the hope that God will vindicate her in the future. But who is this Israel who will be vindicated? Is it all Jews, or only some? Can one tell in the present who precisely will be vindicated when God finally acts in fulfilment of his righteousness, of his covenant obligations? Yes, reply many Jews of Paul's day. The present sign of our future vindication consists in our present loyalty to the covenant obligations laid upon us by our God. Our 'works of the law' demonstrate in the present that, when God acts, we will be seen to be his people. Thus there arises that theology of 'justification by works' which Paul was at such pains to demolish. This is the discussion to which we shall return in the next chapter. For the moment, we must stay with the theme of God's righteousness. Has Paul really used it with the consistency that I have been implying?

Options for a Key Term

Despite the quite clear background to the term within Judaism, a great many readers of Paul have supposed that it meant something quite different. The phrase 'the righteousness of God' does, of course, leave itself open to different interpretations, just as the phrase 'the love of God' can mean either God's love for us or our love for God. But the discussion of 'the righteousness of God' is more complex than that concerning 'the love of God'. There are at least four quite distinct meanings that the phrase has been given in scholarly discussion.

The twists and turns of these various interpretations get quite complex. But unless one attempts to understand them one will be all at sea when faced with different translations and interpretations of one of the most central and important features of Paul's thought. The problem, actually, is not unlike the feelings of someone who, having driven cars for years, is introduced for the first time to what actually goes in the carburettor. How can such an odd little machine have anything to do with driving down the road? The wise mechanic, faced with this question, might attempt simply to demonstrate what happens when the carburettor is working as opposed to what happens when it isn't. This is the sort of exercise upon which we are now embarked.

The basic distinction here is between those who see 'the righteousness of God' as referring to God's own righteousness, and those who see it as referring to a status of righteousness which humans have before God. The accompanying diagram (opposite) has the first of these as its upper half (A), and the second as its lower half (B). The further subdivisions are also important. I begin with the lower half, which has been very popular, not least in Protestant and evangelical circles.

Ever since Martin Luther, many Christians have celebrated the phrase 'the righteousness of God' as denoting that status which humans have, on the basis of faith, as a result of the gospel. But there are two quite different ways of understanding this, reflected in various translations and commentaries. First (B1), one can suppose this 'righteousness' to be the status which Christians are given, granted, or reckoned by or from God. The genitive in question is here a genitive of *origin* ('the righteousness which *comes from* God'). Alternatively (B2), many have read the phrase as an *objective* genitive, which means that the word 'righteousness' is somehow being construed in terms of a quality which *counts before* God, or which *avails with* God.

'Righteousness of God' – Options for interpretation

A. God's own 'righteousness'	**A1.** Righteousness as a moral quality ('of God' as a *possessive* genitive)	**A1a.** 'distributive justice'
		A1b. 'covenant faithfulness'
	A2. Righteousness as God's salvation-creating power ('of God' as a *subjective* genitive)	**A2a.** acts of covenant faithfulness
		A2b. non-covenantal world-defeating actions
B. A 'righteousness' given to humans	**B1.** Righteousness as a righteous standing 'from God' ('of God' as a genitive of *origin*)	**B1a.** 'imputed righteousness'
		B1b. 'imparted righteousness'
	B2. Righteousness as a quality 'which comes before God' or 'avails with God' ('of God' as an *objective* genitive)	**B2a.** a natural quality recognized by God
		B2b. a special gift from God, then recognized as such

In each case, there are further important subdivisions. If the righteousness is something humans have 'from God', is it 'imputed' to them (B1a) – that is, 'reckoned' to be theirs, almost as a legal fiction? Or is it 'imparted' (B1b), given as an actual entity or property, given by God breathing into his people that 'righteousness' which he longs to see? This question has been endlessly debated for hundreds of years, and obviously depends on two quite different meanings of 'righteousness': the first sees it as a *status*, the second as a *quality*.

If the righteousness is something which 'counts before' God, or 'avails with' God, there is again a further question. Is it (B2a) a quality which some humans simply have, by (as we would say) the light of nature? Is it, for instance, the case that some humans simply believe in God, and that God, casting around to see who's who, says to himself 'Yes! That's the "righteousness" I'm looking for?' Was this what happened in the case of Abraham? Or (B2b) does God first somehow give to humans the quality of which he then approves? Is this 'righteousness', then, a natural quality, or a special gift from God?

Many readers will find these twists and turns ridiculously logic-chopping and complex. How can serious theology descend to such intricacies? Again, remember the car and the carburettor. I have met each of these variations, and actually various muddled combinations of them as well, in scholarly and popular writings on Paul, especially on the letter to the Romans. They determine how one reads some of the most vital and central texts he wrote.

Moving up to the first segment, we begin with those who think (A1) that 'righteousness' is a moral *quality* in God. The genitive 'of God' is then simply a possessive genitive; this is a quality which God simply possesses. Second (A2), some think that 'righteousness' denotes God's saving *activity*. The genitive 'of God' then becomes subjective, since it denotes the subject of the implied verb.

These two categories then break down further. If righteousness is a moral quality in God, what sort of a quality might it be? Notoriously, Luther grew up believing (A1a) that God's righteousness was his 'distributive justice', that is, God's moral activity of punishing evil and rewarding virtue. If you read Paul in Latin, as Luther did, that is the impression you would probably get from the word *iustitia*. The second option (A1b), which is the one I want to commend, is to see the quality in question as God's faithfulness to his promises, to his covenant. Before we can pursue this further, we must finish the picture.

102

The idea of righteousness as God's saving activity breaks down, likewise, into two. The second of these (A2b), the one proposed by the influential German scholar Ernst Käsemann, is to see the phrase as a technical term meaning 'God's salvation-creating power', without reference to the covenant, to Israel, to Abraham or to the biblical promises. Käsemann deliberately splits this meaning off from anything 'covenantal', since he wants to emphasize that God's salvation-creating power addresses – indeed, conquers – the whole world, not just Israel. But the first (A2a), which goes very closely with A1b, is to see the phrase denoting precisely the actions which embody God's covenant faithfulness. As we have seen, when the God of Israel fulfils the covenant, this was always designed as the means by which he would address and solve the problems of the world, the whole cosmos.

How are we to decide between these multiple competing options? Despite the long popularity of the lower half of the diagram (B), the overwhelming weight of Jewish evidence, including many passages in scripture that Paul either quotes or alludes to, pushes us decisively into the upper half of the diagram (A). 'The righteousness of God' must refer to God's own righteousness. The Jewish context, in fact, creates such a strong presumption in favour of this that it could only be overthrown if Paul quite clearly argued against it; and, as I shall show, this is not at all the case.

How do we choose between the different options in (A)? We may rule out the old idea of the *iustitia distributiva* (A1a) as a Latin irrelevance. We may also rule out the new suggestion of Käsemann (A2b) as an ingenious impossibility (the texts he quotes in favour of this specialized and technical sense don't in fact mean what he says they mean). We are left, therefore, with the two closely related senses (A1b, A2a) which have to do with God's covenant faithfulness, both as a quality in God and as an active power which goes out, in expression of that faithfulness, to do what the covenant always promised: to deal with evil, to save his people, and to do so with true impartiality. I believe, in fact, that our neat grammatical distinction here between possessive and subjective genitive does not quite do justice to what Paul is getting at here, and that we should probably erase the line that separates these two senses. Since, for Paul, God is the creator, always active within his world, we should expect, in the nature of the case, to find his attributes and his actions belonging extremely closely together.

The test case for all this, of course, is the text of the letters; more especially, Romans itself.

'God's Righteousness' in Paul's Letters

Philippians and 2 Corinthians

Romans is the letter where 'the righteousness of God' forms a major theme. Before we get to it, there are two other passages which are interesting but not decisive for the argument. In Philippians 3:9, a passage often quoted in this discussion, Paul declares that his desire is to gain Christ,

> and be found in him, not having a righteousness of my own, that which is from the law, but that which is through faith in Christ [or: 'through the faithfulness of Christ'], the righteousness from God that is upon faith.

The key phrase here, importantly, is not *dikaiosune theou*, 'God's righteousness', but *dikaiosune ek theou*, a righteousness *from* God. All too often scholars have referred to this passage as though it could be the yardstick for uses of *dikaiosune theou*; but this is impossible. Thinking back to the Hebrew law court, what we have here is the 'righteousness', the status, which the vindicated party possesses as a result of the court's decision. This is 'a righteous status *from God*'; and this is not, as we saw, God's own righteousness.

In 2 Corinthians 5:20-21, a famous text much beloved of Martin Luther, Paul rounds off his argument about his own apostolic commission:

> We are ambassadors for Christ, as though God were making his appeal through us. We appeal on behalf of Christ, 'be reconciled to God'. God made him to be sin for us, who knew no sin, so that in him we might become the *dikaiosune theou*.

I have left the last, critical phrase untranslated. This time it is certainly 'the righteousness of God'; and generations of readers have taken it to be clear evidence for a sense in the lower half of the diagram, most likely B1a. I have pointed out in detail elsewhere, however, that Paul is not talking about justification, but about his own apostolic ministry; that he has already described this in chapter 3 as the ministry of the new covenant; that the point at issue is the fact that apostles are ambassadors of Christ, with God making his appeal through them; and that therefore the apostolic ministry, including its suffering, fear and apparent failure, is itself *an incarnation of the covenant faithfulness of God*. What Paul is saying is that he and his fellow apostles, in their suffering and fear, their faithful witness against all the odds, are not just talking about God's faithfulness; they are actually embodying it. The death of the Messiah has taken care of their apparent failure; now, in him, they *are* 'the righteousness of God', the living embodiment of the message they proclaim.

This reading of 2 Corinthians 5:21 ties the verse so closely in to the whole surrounding context that it thereby demonstrates its correctness. If, however, you insist on reading 2 Corinthians 5:21 with a meaning in the second half of the diagram – presumably B1a, 'imputed righteousness' – you will find, as many commentators have, that it detaches itself from the rest of the chapter and context, as though it were a little floating saying which Paul just threw in here for good measure. The proof of the theory is in the sense it makes when we bring it back to the actual letter.

What then about Romans? This is where *dikaiosune theou* finds its fullest exposition in Paul. Three passages, each of them at crucial stages in the overall argument, come up for particular consideration.

Romans 3

We may leave for a moment the introductory phrase in Romans 1:17 ('in the gospel, God's righteousness is revealed'). Precisely because this is introductory, it is necessarily cryptic, and needs to be interpreted in the light of what comes later. Chapter 3 is where the theme becomes visible, central and vital.

At the start of chapter 3, Paul wrestles with the question posed by the end of chapter 2. God (he has just argued) has now renewed his covenant, and has done so with a community in which Jews and Gentiles belong together, in which the badge of circumcision is irrelevant. Does this mean that God has forgotten his covenant promises to the Jews themselves? In this context, verse 5 clearly refers to God's own righteousness:

> If our unrighteousness serves to establish God's righteousness, is God unjust to punish?

The meaning of 'righteousness' is closely related to the idea of God's faithfulness or unfaithfulness in the immediately preceding verses. The verses in question clearly have to do with the vocation of Israel, with God's purposes for Israel, and with Israel's failure to fulfil those purposes. This is what we may call 'covenant theology'; in this context, 'God's righteousness' most naturally means 'God's covenant faithfulness'.

Paul does not abandon this theme in the second half of the chapter, where in a few short verses he lays out the heart of his message.

> But now, apart from the law, God's righteousness has been revealed, witnessed by the law and the prophets. It is the righteousness of God, through the faithfulness of Jesus Christ, for all who believe. For there is no distinction: for all sinned, and came short of God's glory, and are justified freely by his grace, through the redemption which is in Christ Jesus. God put him forth as a means of atonement, through faith, by means of his blood. This was to demonstrate his righteousness, through the passing over of former sins in the forbearance of God. It was to demonstrate his righteousness in the present time, so that he might himself be righteous and the justifier of the person who has faith in Jesus. (Romans 3:21-26)

We recall that 'justify', 'justifier' and 'justification' have, in Greek, the same root as 'righteous' and 'righteousness'. What, then, is going on here?

By the time we reach verse 20 of chapter 3, Paul has demonstrated not only that the Gentile world is out of touch with its creator God, and in consequence under judgment, but also that the Jews, too, despite being given the covenant through which God intended to redeem the world, have failed in their task. All humankind is thus in the dock in God's metaphorical law court. In terms of the law-court diagram, it is no longer the case of Israel coming before God as the plaintiff, bringing a charge against the pagans. Gentile and Jew alike are now guilty defendants. In terms of the covenant scenario for which the law-court scene is the vital metaphor, God intended to be faithful to his covenant, his intention was to vindicate Israel and so to save the whole world, *through* the faithfulness of Israel; but Israel as a whole were faithless. What is God to do?

Paul's answer is that the Messiah, King Jesus, has been the true, faithful Israelite. Underneath the dense theology of the passage just quoted stands Paul's central gospel scene: the death and resurrection of Jesus, seen as the point at which, and the means by which, God's covenant purposes for Israel, that is, his intention to deal once and for all with the sin of the world, would finally be accomplished. God has dealt with sin in the cross of Jesus; he has now vindicated Jesus by raising him from the dead. 'The faithfulness of Jesus' (which later, in Romans 5, Paul can also refer to as 'the obedience of Jesus') is thus *the means whereby the righteousness of God is revealed*. God is himself righteous, as the covenant God who has made promises and kept them. In terms of the law-court metaphor, he has been true to his word, he has been impartial (note the way in which Paul goes on at once to speak of God's even-handed dealing with Jew and Gentile alike), and he has dealt with sin. He has also thereby vindicated the helpless: he is 'the justifier of the one who has faith'. This theme of God's own righteousness, understood as his covenant faithfulness, and seen in terms of the law-court metaphor, is the key to this vital passage.

Paul stresses, by repetition, the underlying point: the gospel of Jesus reveals God's righteousness, in that God is himself righteous, and, as part of that, God is the one who declares the believer to be righteous. Once again we must insist that there is of course a 'righteous' standing, a status, which human beings have as a result of God's gracious verdict in Christ. Paul is perfectly happy with that. We shall consider it in the next chapter. But Paul *does not use the phrase 'God's righteousness' to denote it*. God's righteousness is God's own righteousness. In this crucial passage in Romans 3, he shows how God has been righteous in all the senses we outlined earlier. He has been true to the covenant, which always aimed to deal with the sin of the world; he has kept his promises; he has dealt with sin on the cross; he has done so impartially, making a way of salvation for Jew and Gentile alike; and he now, as the righteous judge, helps and saves the helpless who cast themselves on his mercy. If you give to any of the occurrences of the phrase *dikaiosune theou* in this passage a meaning other than some combination of A1b and A2a (as many translations do), the whole thing will get muddled. If you leave it clearly referring to these senses throughout, everything becomes clear.

Were there more space, we could go on to show how Paul then broadens the perspective out, to reveal in chapter 4 that what God has done in Christ was all along the meaning and intention behind the promises made to Abraham in Genesis 15, the great covenant chapter in which God promised him a worldwide family characterized by faith. Romans 3:21 – 4:25 as a whole expounds and celebrates God's own righteousness, God's covenant faithfulness, revealed, unveiled, in the great apocalyptic events of the death and resurrection of Jesus Christ.

Romans 9–10

This then sets us up for a clear reading of Romans 9–10, the other crucial passage for the meaning of *dikaiosune theou*. Again, the word 'righteousness' often, confusingly for us, denotes that status which the people of God now have; but this is not God's own righteousness. The vital passage is 10:2-4:

> I bear [my fellow Jews] witness that they have a zeal for God; but it is not according to knowledge. For, being ignorant of God's righteousness, and seeking to establish their own righteousness, they did not submit to God's righteousness. For Christ is the end of the law, so that all who have faith may be justified.

This passage in fact sums up the whole argument of 9:6-39, where, though the phrase 'God's righteousness' does not occur, the whole discussion is about whether God has in fact been righteous, has in fact kept his covenant promises, and if so how. We must beware of thinking that the idea is present only when the phrase occurs; the whole context is about nothing else than God's righteousness. Israel, says Paul, is ignorant of what God has righteously and faithfully been doing in her history. In seeking to establish a status of righteousness, of covenant membership, which will be for Jews and Jews only, she has not submitted to God's righteousness. The covenant always envisaged a worldwide family; Israel, clinging to her own special status as the covenant-bearer, has betrayed the purpose for which that covenant was made. It is as though the postman were to imagine that all the letters in his bag were intended for him.

When Paul says that Israel 'did not submit to the righteousness of God', he is clearly referring back to Romans 3:21-26, the passage we looked at a moment ago. There, as we saw, Paul declared that 'the righteousness of God' had been revealed in the gospel of Jesus Christ, the gospel which declares that God has one way of salvation for all, Jew and Gentile alike. When Paul's fellow Jews rejected Jesus (as Paul did himself to begin with), and when they continue to reject the message about Jesus which Paul proclaims, he sees the underlying reason: they recognize, as he has had to recognize, that it will mean abandoning the idea of a covenant membership which will be inalienably hers and hers alone. So the great argument of Romans 9–11 goes on its way, reaching at its climax the most significant statement, quoting from Jeremiah 31:33 and Isaiah 27:9 – this will be my covenant with them, when I take away their sins (Romans 11:27). As I have argued in more detail elsewhere, Paul holds firmly to the hope that the renewal of the covenant which has taken place in Jesus the Messiah will be effective not only for Gentiles but also for Jews who will come, as he himself has done, to faith in Jesus as the Jewish Messiah.

Romans 1:17

We thus return to Romans 1:16-17 in the hope of being able to understand it at last.

> For I am not ashamed of the gospel; for it is God's power for salvation to all who believe, the Jew first and also the Greek. For God's righteousness is revealed in it, from faith to faith, as it is written: 'The righteous shall live by faith.'

This tight-packed statement is what Paul then gradually unpacks throughout much of the rest of the letter, and we must therefore understand it in the light of our reading of what follows.

Paul is explaining why he is eager to announce the gospel, the royal proclamation of King Jesus as Lord of the world, throughout the world and particularly at Rome itself. The gospel, he says, reveals or unveils God's own righteousness, his covenant faithfulness, which operates through the faithfulness of Jesus Christ for the benefit of all those who in turn are faithful ('from faith to faith'). In other words, when Paul announces that Jesus Christ is Lord, the Lord of the world, he is in that very act and announcement unveiling before the world the great news that the one God of all the world has been true to his word, has dealt decisively with the evil that has invaded his creation, and is now restoring justice, peace and truth.

This is the fundamental thing that Paul wants the Roman church, and indeed the whole world, to grasp. What happened in the events concerning Jesus was not a puzzling or peculiar turn of circumstances, but was the outworking of God's age-old plan and purpose. If the church in Rome can grasp this, they will be in exactly the right position both to support the urgent missionary work which must now take place, and to live as the one people of God, putting aside their cultural distinctions so that they can worship and serve the one God as brothers and sisters. This points already to the rich doctrine of justification and community which I shall be exploring in the next chapter. 'Covenant' and 'apocalyptic' belong together in this great sweep of thought: the message about King Jesus unveils the true

God in all his glory as the covenant-keeping God, the God who has at last dealt with sin. Over against all the powers of the world, not least those in Rome itself, the true God is revealed as the one Lord of all the earth. And Paul is not ashamed to say so.

Conclusion: The God of Israel and of the World

I have argued throughout this chapter and chapter 4 that Paul re-thought the very meaning of the word 'God' by means of Jesus and the Spirit. There is one great theme which I have not explicitly mentioned, but which I now wish in conclusion to unveil, so to speak, as the very heart of this whole rethinking on Paul's part.

Paul speaks, in one of the speeches in Acts, of 'the gospel of the grace of God' (Acts 20:24). This is, after all, the great theme of the greatest of the letters, which we have studied very briefly in the present chapter. Romans is often regarded as an exposition of judicial, or law-court, theology. But that is a mistake. The law court forms a vital metaphor at a key stage of the argument. But at the heart of Romans we find a theology of love.

We have seen continually that Paul's redefinition, his fresh understanding, of the one true God came especially through his grasp of the fact that this God was revealed supremely in Jesus, and there supremely in the cross. If we leave the notion of 'righteousness' as a law-court metaphor only, as so many have done in the past, this gives the impression of a legal transaction, a cold piece of business, almost a trick of thought performed by a God who is logical and correct but hardly one we would want to worship. But if we understand 'God's righteousness', as I have tried to do, in terms of the covenant faithfulness of God, then there is of course one word which sums up that whole train of thought, and which for Paul perfectly describes the God he knows in Jesus Christ and by the Spirit. In Romans 5 and 8, drawing together the threads of the argument so far, he says that the cross of Jesus reveals supremely the *love* of God (5:6-11; 8:31-39). If you understand *dikaiosune theou* in the way I have suggested, you cannot play off justice and love against one another. God's justice is his love in action, to right the wrongs of his suffering world by taking their weight upon himself. God's love is the driving force of his justice, so that it can never become a blind or

110

arbitrary thing, a cold system which somehow God operates, or which operates God. Because the gospel reveals this covenant love, this covenant faithfulness, of the living God, Paul knows that whatever happens the future is secure. He can announce the gospel in the face of the powers of the world, and they can do their worst to him. The death and resurrection of Jesus have unveiled the faithful love of God, and nothing can separate him from it:

> For I am persuaded that neither death nor life, nor angels, nor rulers, nor things present, nor things to come, nor powers, nor height, nor depth, nor any other creature shall be able to separate us from the love of God in Christ Jesus our Lord. (Romans 8:38-39)

The language of theology, properly understood, gives birth to the language of love. Paul has no problem about a split between head and heart, or between right-brain and left-brain. He has grasped the truth that the one true God is now made known in Jesus and the Spirit. And, grasping that, he knows that he is himself grasped, held, sustained and saved by the faithful love of the faithful God.

But if the true God is as Paul has now perceived him, revealed in Jesus Christ and in the Spirit, this means that Paul's knowledge of this God can never be a private thing. It is something that by its very nature is shared with a whole community, and flows into a new vocation. How he conceived of this community, its origin, its nature, and its defining unity, and how he conceived of this vocation, this mission – that is the question of justification. And that will be the subject of the next chapter.

CHAPTER 7

Justification and the Church

What is 'Justification'?

Many people, including many supposedly 'Pauline' Christians, would say, off the cuff, that the heart of Paul's teaching is 'justification by faith'. What many such people understand as the meaning of this phrase is something like this. People are always trying to pull themselves up by their own moral bootstraps. They try to save themselves by their own efforts; to make themselves good enough for God, or for heaven. This doesn't work; one can only be saved by the sheer unmerited grace of God, appropriated not by good works but by faith. This account of justification owes a good deal both to the controversy between Pelagius and Augustine in the early fifth century and to that between Erasmus and Luther in the early sixteenth century.

In the present chapter I shall suggest that this popular view of 'justification by faith', though not entirely misleading, does not do justice to the richness and precision of Paul's doctrine, and indeed distorts it at various points. I shall then suggest a more appropriate way of connecting Paul's 'gospel', which we discussed in chapter 3, and the full Pauline meaning of 'justification'. Briefly and baldly put, if you start with the popular view of justification, you may actually lose sight of the heart of the Pauline gospel; whereas if you start with the Pauline gospel itself you will get justification in all its glory thrown in as well. To address these issues we need to remind ourselves again of one aspect of recent Pauline scholarship.

The traditional questions of Pauline theology, as we saw in the first chapter, have been knocked into quite a new shape by what we have come to call 'the Sanders revolution'. Since the publication in 1977 of Ed Sanders' *Paul and Palestinian Judaism*, the fat has been in the fire. Everything we knew about Paul, or thought we knew, has had to be re-examined. Sanders argued, basically, that the normal Christian, and especially Protestant, readings of Paul were seriously flawed, because they attributed to first-century Judaism theological views which belonged rather to medieval Catholicism. Once we described Judaism accurately, Sanders argued, we were forced to rethink Paul's critique of it, and his whole positive theology in its turn.

There has been a knee-jerk acceptance of Sanders in certain quarters, particularly where he has been seen as an ally in the broader Enlightenment project of demolishing the historical roots of orthodox Christianity. Equally, there has been a knee-jerk rejection of Sanders by those desperately concerned to maintain the orthodoxy they knew and loved, and defend it against critical attack. Most of us in the guild of New Testament studies have, I think, taken the path – surely the path of wisdom – of searching the texts carefully to see if, and if so to what extent, these things may be so. It is to that kind of exercise that this chapter is devoted.

One of the many odd things about Sanders' presentation of Paul is that he continues to accept what the tradition has told us Paul meant by 'justification' itself. Since he has redrawn so many other aspects of Paul's thought, one might have supposed he would take a fresh look at this too; but he doesn't. He contents himself with a modified version of the thesis made famous at the start of the century by Wrede and Schweitzer: that justification is not the centre of Paul's thought, but rather takes a secondary, and essentially ad hoc and polemical, place to what Schweitzer called 'Christ-mysticism' and what Sanders calls 'participation'. But he continues to assume that, when Paul does speak of justification and its various cognates, he is talking about what the tradition – including the Lutheran tradition that Sanders has so strongly criticized – supposed he was talking about.

I wish to suggest that this is not, in fact, the case. In terms of the *place* of justification within Paul's thought, I have already indicated that it cannot be put right at the centre, since that place is already taken by the person of Jesus himself, and the gospel announcement of his sovereign kingship. But this does not mean that justification becomes a secondary, still less an inessential, matter. Let it not be assumed that I am agreeing with Wrede or Schweitzer. Rather, when we understand exactly what Paul did mean by 'justification', we will come to see that it is organically and integrally linked to what he meant by 'the gospel'. It cannot be detached without pulling part of the very heart of Paul away with it. This claim, however, does not of itself indicate what 'justification' actually is. It simply clears the ground for our further exploration.

We saw in an earlier chapter that 'the gospel' has come to mean various things which are not precisely what Paul meant by it. We now discover that the same is true of 'justification'. The discussions of justification in much of the history of the church, certainly since Augustine, got off on the wrong foot – at least in terms of understanding Paul – and they have stayed there ever since. Interestingly, Alister McGrath, in his monumental history of the doctrine, allows right from the start for exactly this possibility. 'The doctrine of justification', he writes,

> has come to develop a meaning quite independent of its biblical origins, and concerns the means by which man's relationship to God is established. The church has chosen to subsume its discussion of the reconciliation of man to God under the aegis of justification, thereby giving the concept an emphasis quite absent from the New Testament. The 'doctrine of justification' has come to bear a meaning within dogmatic theology which is quite independent of its Pauline origins...

So far, I basically agree; and I shall develop the detail of this from the Pauline end, which McGrath himself does not do. But he continues:

> Even if it could be shown that [justification] plays a minimal role in Pauline soteriology, or that its origins lie in an anti-Judaising polemic quite inappropriate to the theological circumstances of today, its significance would not be diminished as a result.[1]

McGrath, clearly, is seeking to side-step potential rejoinders to his project from pesky Pauline specialists grumbling that the whole discussion is based on a mistake. As an historian, he is completely entitled to do this. Whatever Paul meant by a word, if the church has used that word or its equivalents in other languages to mean something else for nearly two thousand years, that is neither here nor there. But a problem remains none the less. In all the church's discussions of what has come to be called 'justification' (which as McGrath says may not be what Paul meant by the term), Paul himself is of course constantly invoked. His letters are ransacked for statements, dare we say even for proof-texts, on a subject which he may not himself have conceived in those terms. If it is true that Paul meant by 'justification' something which is significantly different from what subsequent debate has meant, then this appeal to him is consistently flawed, maybe even invalidated altogether. If we are to understand Paul himself, and perhaps to provide a Pauline critique of current would-be biblical theology and agendas, it is therefore vital and, I believe, urgent, that we ask whether such texts have in fact been misused. The answer to that question, I suggest, is an emphatic Yes.

The church's 'doctrine of justification', says McGrath, addresses 'the question of how the saving action of God towards mankind in Christ may be appropriated by the individual'. That is to say, it deals with 'the question of what man must do if he is to enter into a relationship with God through Christ'; moreover, it also concerns itself with establishing 'the presuppositions and consequences' of this event.[2] Classically, this doctrine ever since Augustine has been concerned with warding off some version or other of the Pelagian heresy. Different people have meant different things by that heresy, and the sharp-eyed have spotted it, sometimes, even in those who thought they were opposing it root and branch. I must insist, right away, that if you come upon anyone who genuinely thinks that they can fulfil Pelagius' programme, in whichever form or variation you like, you should gently but firmly set them right. There is simply no way that human beings can make themselves fit for the presence or salvation of God. What is more, I know of no serious theologian, Protestant, Catholic or Orthodox, who thinks otherwise; indeed, one of the best expositions of the Augustinian or Lutheran or Calvinist doctrine of justification I have ever heard was given by a Jesuit, Father Edward Yarnold, in an ecumenical meeting. If Pelagius survives at all today, it is at the level of popular secular moralism, which is in any case becoming harder and harder to find in the Western world.

But if we come to Paul with these questions in mind – the questions about how human beings come into a living and saving relationship with the living and saving God – it is not justification that springs to his lips or pen. When he describes how persons, finding themselves confronted with the act of God in Christ, come to appropriate that act for themselves, he has a clear train of thought, repeated at various points. The message about Jesus and his cross and resurrection – 'the gospel', in terms of our previous chapters – is announced to them; through this means, God works by his Spirit upon their hearts; as a result, they come to believe the message; they join the Christian community through baptism, and begin to share in its common life and its common way of life. That is how people come into relationship with the living God.

If you say that this is what you mean by justification by faith, I reply that we must take note of the fact that when Paul is setting out this train of thought, as he does (for instance) in 1 Thessalonians 1, he does not mention justification. That is not what he is talking about. If you respond that the entire epistle to the Romans is a description of how persons become Christians, and that justification is central there, I will answer, anticipating my later argument, that this way of reading Romans has systematically done violence to that text for hundreds of years, and that it is time for the text itself to be heard again. Paul does indeed discuss the subject-matter which the church has referred to as 'justification', but he does not use 'justification' language for it. This alerts us to the negative truth of McGrath's point. Paul may or may not agree with Augustine, Luther or anyone else about how people come to a personal knowledge of God in Christ; but *he does not use the language of 'justification' to denote this event or process.* Instead, he speaks of the proclamation of the gospel of Jesus, the work of the spirit, and the entry into the common life of the people of God.

What then *does* Paul mean when he uses the language of 'justification', and how is this related to the gospel? I shall now argue for a threefold position about justification language in Paul, corresponding closely to the threefold grid I offered in the previous chapter for understanding 'God's righteousness'.

First, it is *covenant* language — not in the sense of that word made famous through some sixteenth- and seventeenth-century discussions, but in the first-century Jewish sense. When Paul speaks of justification he is operating within the whole world of thought of second-temple Judaism, which clung onto the covenant promises in the face of increasingly difficult political circumstances.

Second, it is *law-court* language, functioning within the covenantal setting as a strong explanatory metaphor. Two things must be said about this. First, this metaphor is necessary for understanding what the covenant was all about. The covenant was there to put the world to rights, to deal with evil and to restore God's justice and order to the cosmos. Second, it is never independent of the covenant setting. It cannot be made into an absolute and free-standing concept without doing violence both to itself and to the fundamental meaning of the covenant.

Third, justification for Paul cannot be understood apart from *eschatology*.

It cannot, that is, be made into an abstract or timeless system, a method of salvation to be randomly applied. It is part of the Pauline worldview in which the creator of the world has acted, uniquely, climactically and decisively, in Jesus Christ, for the rescue of the entire cosmos, and is now, by his Spirit, bringing all things into subjection to this Jesus.

How does this work out in detail? To answer this we must take another step backwards, this time into Paul's own Jewish world.

Justification in Paul's Jewish Context

I have already outlined the worldview and agenda of Saul of Tarsus. He was, by his own admission, a zealous Pharisee, close in his views to the out-and-out revolutionaries. As such, Saul was not interested in a timeless system of salvation, whether of works-righteousness or anything else. He wanted God to redeem Israel. Moreover, he drew freely on texts from the Hebrew Bible which promised that Israel's God would do exactly that. People like Saul were not primarily interested in the state of their souls after death; that was no doubt important, but no doubt God would have the matter in hand. They were interested, urgently, in the salvation which, they believed, the one true God had promised to his people Israel.

One feature of this hope needs to be emphasized at this point. *The purpose of the covenant was never simply that the creator wanted to have Israel as a special people, irrespective of the fate of the rest of the world.* The covenant was there to deal with the sin, and bring about the salvation, of the world. It was therefore utterly appropriate, as I said earlier, that this great event should be described in terms drawn from the setting in which evil was regularly dealt with, namely that of the law court. As we saw in the previous chapter, God himself was seen as the judge; evildoers (i.e. the Gentiles, and renegade Jews) would finally be judged and punished; God's faithful people (i.e. Israel, or at least the true Israelites) would be vindicated. Their redemption, which would take the physical and concrete form of political liberation, the restoration of the Temple, and ultimately of resurrection itself, would be seen as the great law-court showdown, the great victory before the great judge.

This 'justification' would thus also be *eschatological*: it would be the final fulfilment of Israel's long-cherished hope. But, importantly, this event could be *anticipated* under certain circumstances, so that particular Jews and/or groups of Jews could see themselves as the true Israel in advance of the day when everyone else would see them thus as well. Those who adhered in the proper way to the ancestral covenant charter, the Torah, were assured in the present that they were the people who would be vindicated in the future. This scheme is clearest, I think, at Qumran, not least in the recently published scroll that goes by the name of 4QMMT. There, 'justification by works' has nothing to do with individual Jews attempting a kind of proto-Pelagian pulling themselves up by their moral bootstraps, and everything to do with the definition of the true Israel in advance of the final eschatological showdown. Justification in this setting, then, is not a matter of *how someone enters the community of the true people of God*, but of *how you tell who belongs to that community*, not least in the period of time before the eschatological event itself, when the matter will become public knowledge.

I have, of course, foreshortened discussion of these difficult and contentious matters a great deal. But already it should be clear that certain aspects of the post-Augustine debate of what has come to be called 'justification' have nothing much to do with the context in which Paul was writing. 'Justification' in the first century was not about how someone might establish a relationship with God. It was about God's eschatological definition, both future and present, of who was, in fact, a member of his people. In Sanders' terms, it was not so much about 'getting in', or indeed about 'staying in', as about 'how you could tell who was in'. In standard Christian theological language, it wasn't so much about soteriology as about ecclesiology; not so much about salvation as about the church.

Already we can see that this brief study of the Jewish meaning of 'justification' emphasizes two points I made in the last chapter. First, within the law-court setting, the 'righteousness' which someone has when the court has found in their favour is not a moral quality which they bring into court with them; it is the legal status which they carry out of court with them. Second, we saw that this legal status, the 'righteousness' of the person who has won the case, is not to be confused with the judge's 'righteousness'. These implications have, ironically, been missed often enough by the very theologians who have tried to insist on the forensic (law court) nature of the doctrine.

The first-century context also indicates that the modern scholarly discussions of justification from Wrede and Schweitzer to the present day have likewise very often been beside the point. Schweitzer's dichotomy of the law court and of 'Christ-mysticism', Sanders' similar dichotomy of 'juristic' and 'participationist' categories, and many other similar schemes, have missed the really central matter. With Sanders this is all the more ironic, since he sees and argues for in Judaism what he misses in Paul: the covenant. Once you understand how first-century Jewish covenant theology actually works, you will see that law-court language, 'participation' language, and a great deal else besides, settle down and make their home with each other, dovetailed without confusion and distinguished without dislocation. But to take this further we must turn, at last, to Paul. What, precisely, does Paul mean by 'justification', and how does it relate to what he meant by 'the gospel'?

Justification in Paul's Christian Theology

There is of course easily enough material on what Paul meant by justification to occupy another whole book. All there is space for here is to highlight certain features, raise some key questions, and make a few suggestions. I shall follow the time-honoured, and methodologically justifiable, process of discussing the letters in what I believe is their chronological order, and then trying to pull some threads together.

Galatians

Despite a long tradition to the contrary, the problem Paul addresses in Galatians is not the question of how precisely someone becomes a Christian, or attains to a relationship with God. (I'm not even sure how Paul would express, in Greek, our notion of 'relationship with God', but we'll leave that aside.) The problem he addresses is: should his ex-pagan converts be circumcised or not? Now this question is by no means obviously to do with the questions faced by Augustine and Pelagius, or by Luther and Erasmus. On anyone's reading, but especially within its first-century context, it has to do quite obviously with the question of how you *define the people of God*: are they to be defined by the badges of Jewish race, or in some other way? Circumcision is not a 'moral' issue; it does not have to do with moral effort, or earning salvation by good deeds. Nor can we simply treat it as a religious ritual, then designate all religious ritual as crypto-Pelagian good works, and so smuggle Pelagius into Galatia as the arch-opponent after all. First-century thought, both Jewish and Christian, simply doesn't work like that.

How then does the argument of Galatians, especially in the crucial chapters 2–4, run? The question at issue in the church at Antioch, to which Paul refers in chapter 2, is not how people came to a relationship with God, but who one is allowed to eat with. Who is a member of the people of God? Are ex-pagan converts full members or not? Within this question, which Paul clearly regards as a paradigm for the issues facing the Galatians themselves, certain things stand out.

First, the context is irrevocably covenantal. Galatians 3 is a lengthy exposition of the family of Abraham, focused initially on the covenant chapter, Genesis 15, and moving through various other covenantal passages, not least from Deuteronomy 27. In discussing Abraham, Paul is not simply producing a powerful string of proof-texts. He is going back to the actual subject, which is not how individuals, Abraham then and the Galatians now, come to faith (as we say), but rather the question of who belongs to Abraham's family. This is clear in 3:29, where the conclusion of the argument is not 'if you are Abraham's family, you are in Christ', but the other way round. God established the family of Abraham. Paul reaffirms it. What matters is who belongs to it. Paul says that all those in Christ belong, whatever their racial background.

Further, Paul's argument cuts right across the traditional twentieth-century scholarly battle-lines. If you concentrate on Romans, and shut half an eye as you do so, you can just about get away with treating chapters 1–4 as (in Sanders' language) 'juridical' and 5–8 as 'participationist'. The first part, from that point of view, is about 'Justification'; the second, about 'being in Christ'. But in Galatians the two categories are happily jumbled up together, not least in the last paragraph of chapter 3.

> The law was our overseer until Christ, so that we might be justified by faith. But now that faith has come, we are no longer under the overseer. For you are all children of God, through faith, in Christ Jesus. For as many of you as were baptized into Christ have put on Christ. There is neither Jew nor Greek, neither slave nor free, no male and female: for you are all one in Christ Jesus. And if you are Christ's, you are Abraham's seed, heirs according to the promise.

In particular, the polemic against the Torah in Galatians simply will not work if we 'translate' it into polemic either against straightforward self-help moralism or against the more subtle snare of 'legalism', as some have suggested. The passages about the law only work – and by 'work' I mean they will only make full sense in their contexts, which is what counts in the last analysis – when we take them as references to the Jewish law, the Torah, seen as the national charter of the Jewish race.

Paul does not regard this Torah as a bad thing. He regards it as part of one vital stage in God's secret plan. That stage has now been put into operation, and has been completed. The time has come for a new stage: not that Paul (like the heretic Marcion in the second century) has come to believe that Judaism and the law were evil, or the creation of a lesser god, or anything like that; but that in Christ and by the Spirit the one God is now extending his salvation to all, irrespective of race. That was the message that both Antioch and Galatia needed to hear.

What Paul means by justification, in this context, should therefore be clear. It is not 'how you become a Christian', so much as 'how you can tell who is a member of the covenant family'. When two people share Christian faith, says Paul, they can share table-fellowship, no matter what their ancestry. And all this is based four-square, of course, on the theology of the cross. 'I am crucified with Christ,' he writes, 'nevertheless I live; yet not I, but Christ lives in me' (2:19-20). The cross has obliterated the privileged distinction that Saul of Tarsus supposed himself to enjoy; the new life he has as Paul the apostle is a life defined, not by his old existence, but solely by the crucified and risen Messiah.

The cross, in fact, throughout Galatians, is the redeeming turning-point of history. It is the goal of Israel's strange covenant story. As a result, it is God's way of healing his world. Through the cross, 'the world is crucified to me, and I to the world,' so that now 'neither circumcision nor uncircumcision matters; what matters is new creation' (6:14-16). This is covenant language. Justification, in Galatians, is the doctrine which insists that all who share faith in Christ belong at the same table, no matter what their racial differences, as together they wait for the final new creation.

The Corinthian Correspondence

Before moving to Philippians and then Romans, I should add a Corinthian footnote. I dealt with 2 Corinthians 5:21 in the previous chapter; this time we glance at 1 Corinthians 1:30. There, Paul declares that 'It is by God's doing that you are in Christ Jesus, who became for us wisdom from God, righteousness, sanctification and redemption.' It is difficult to squeeze any precise dogma of justification out of this shorthand summary. It is the only passage I know where something called 'the imputed righteousness of Christ,' a phrase more often found in post-Reformation theology and piety than in the New Testament, finds any basis in the text. But if we are to claim it as such, we must also be prepared to talk of the imputed wisdom of Christ; the imputed sanctification of Christ; and the imputed redemption of Christ; and that, though no doubt they are all true in some overall general sense, will certainly make nonsense of the very specialized and technical senses so frequently given to the phrase 'the righteousness of Christ' in the history of theology. The point Paul is making is the large one, that all the things of which human beings are proud are as nothing before the gospel of the cross of Christ. All that we have that is worth having comes from God and is found in Christ.

Philippians

So to Philippians. Here, verses 2-11 of chapter 3 are the important ones for our purposes, although justification itself is only mentioned in one verse.

> [2] Watch out for the dogs; watch out for the evil-workers; watch out for the mutilated ones. [3] For it is we who are 'the circumcision' — we, who worship God in the Spirit, who boast in King Jesus, and put no confidence in the flesh.
>
> [4] I too, however, do have reason for confidence in the flesh. If anyone else thinks they have confidence in the flesh, I have more: [5] circumcised on the eighth day, of the race of Israel and the tribe of Benjamin, a Hebrew of Hebrews, as to the law a Pharisee, [6] as to zeal a persecutor of the church, as to righteousness in the law blameless.
>
> [7] But whatever gain I had, that I counted loss because of the Messiah. [8] Indeed, I count everything as loss because of the surpassing worth of the knowledge of King Jesus, my Lord, through whom I have suffered the loss of all things, and reckon them as trash, so that I may gain the Messiah, [9] and be found in him — not having a righteousness of my own, from the law, but that which is through the faithfulness of the Messiah, the righteousness from God that comes upon faith: [10] that I may know him and the power of his resurrection, and the fellowship of his sufferings, becoming conformed to his death, [11] if somehow I may attain to the resurrection of the dead.

The context of the letter as a whole is that of Paul's address to a congregation in the pagan Roman colony of Philippi. My tentative reading of this passage runs like this. Paul is putting to the Philippians the possibility that, as he was prepared to abandon all his privileges to gain Christ, so they may have to do the same with theirs. He bases this argument, that they should imitate him, on the poem about Jesus Christ in chapter 2, verses 5-11. There, as we saw in our chapter 4 above, he says that Christ, though in the form of God, did not regard his equality with God as something to exploit, but emptied himself; wherefore God highly exalted him. In this setting, Paul speaks frankly in Philippians 3 about covenant membership, not about a detached system of salvation, nor about the Augustine–Pelagius debate under another name. He is saying, in effect: I, though possessing covenant membership according to the flesh, did not regard that covenant membership as something to exploit; I emptied myself, sharing the death of the Messiah; wherefore God has given me the membership that really counts, in which I too will share the glory of Christ.

How does this work out? Paul first lists his racial covenant privileges, then outlines the features of his new position. The central point in the latter exposition is undoubtedly Christ, not justification, as you will see by a quick count of references: half a dozen or more to Christ, one only to justification.

The critical verse for our purposes is 3:9 ('and be found in him... comes upon faith'). It provides a clear statement of how 'justification' language actually works.

First, it is *membership* language. When Paul says he does not have a righteousness 'of my own', based on Torah, the context of the previous verses must mean that he is speaking of a righteousness, a covenant status, which was his as a Jew by birth, marked with the covenant badge of circumcision, and claiming to be part of the inner circle of that people by being a zealous Pharisee. That which he is refusing in the first half of verse 9 is not a moralistic or self-help righteousness, but the status of orthodox Jewish covenant membership.

Second, the covenant status Paul now enjoys is the gift of God: it is a *dikaiosune ek theou*, a 'righteousness from God'. As we saw earlier, this is not to be confused with the righteousness *of* God, the *dikaiosune theou* itself. God's own righteousness has to do with his own covenant *faithfulness*, and so forth, not with the status he bestows on his people. Paul is here referring to the status of covenant *membership*; it is the gift of God, not something acquired in any way by the human beings involved; and this gift is bestowed

124

upon faith. The place of faith in this picture has long been problematic within post-Reformation dogmatics. Is faith something I 'do' to earn God's favour, and, if not, what role does it play? Once we release Paul's justification-language from the burden of having to describe 'how someone *becomes* a Christian', however, this is simply no longer a problem. There is no danger of imagining that Christian faith is after all a surrogate 'work', let alone a substitute form of moral righteousness. Faith is the badge of covenant membership, not something someone 'performs' as a kind of initiation test.

Think how this works out in practice. As I said earlier, Paul's conception of how people are drawn into salvation starts with the preaching of the gospel, continues with the work of the Spirit in and through that preaching, and the effect of the Spirit's work on the hearts of the hearers, and concludes with the coming to birth of faith, and entry into the family through baptism. 'No one can say "Jesus is Lord" except by the Holy Spirit' (1 Corinthians 12:3). But when that confession is made, God declares that this person, who (perhaps to their own surprise) believes the gospel, is thereby marked out as being within the true covenant family. Justification is not how someone *becomes* a Christian. It is the declaration that they *have become* a Christian. And the total context of this doctrine, here in Philippians 3, is that of the expectation – not of a final salvation in which the individual is abstracted from the present world, but of the final new heavens and new earth, as the Lord comes from the heavenly realm to transform the earthly (3:20-21). Justification belongs within the total covenantal framework, with all its overtones of law court, participation and everything else. It reminds the Philippians that their obligation is now to regard Christ as their contemporaries regarded Caesar: the Lord (*kyrios*) who will become the Saviour (*soter*) – and thus to receive their covenant membership in God's people as a gift, a gift for which even Jewish racial covenant membership, let alone Roman citizenship, is at best an advance sign and at worst a damaging parody.

Romans

So to Romans, where again we shall have to be far briefer than one would ideally like.

Beginning at the beginning, we recapitulate from chapter 3 one of the most important points of all. When Paul says 'the gospel', he does not mean 'justification by faith'; he means the message, the royal announcement, of Jesus Christ as Lord. Romans 1:3-4, as we saw, gives a summary of the content of his gospel; Romans 1:16-17 gives a summary of the *effect*, not the *content*, of the gospel.

> For I am not ashamed of the gospel; for it is God's power for salvation to all who believe, the Jew first and also the Greek. For God's righteousness is revealed in it, from faith to faith, as it is written: 'The righteous shall live by faith'.

This does not, therefore, mean 'the gospel reveals justification by faith as the true scheme of salvation, as opposed to Jewish self-help moralism'. When we unpack it fully, in the light of subsequent passages in the letter, it means:

> The gospel – the announcement of the lordship of Jesus the Messiah – reveals God's righteousness, his covenant faithfulness, his dealing with the sin of the world through the fulfilment of his covenant in this Lord Jesus Christ. He has done all this righteously, that is, impartially. He has dealt with sin, and rescued the helpless. He has thereby fulfilled his promises.

We may note that, though Paul describes God as having acted as the righteous judge in the law court, this is not one metaphor among many. It expresses the heart and purpose of the covenant, namely, to deal with sin and so to save the world. This purpose has now been accomplished in Jesus Christ the Lord.

But how? As the letter progresses, we run into a problem. In many traditions, Romans has been regarded as a book about 'how someone becomes a Christian'. But it isn't at all clear how chapter 2 fits into this scheme. Many commentators and scholars declare themselves baffled.

It is strange, above all, that the first mention of justification in Romans is a mention of justification by *works* – apparently with Paul's approval (2:13: 'It is not the hearers of the law who will be righteous before God, but the doers of the law who will be justified'). The right way to understand this, I believe, is to see that Paul is talking about the *final* justification. Eschatology, the hope of Israel, dominates the horizon as ever. The point is: who will be vindicated, resurrected, shown to be the covenant people, on the last day? Paul's answer, with which many non-Christian Jews would have agreed, is that those who will be vindicated on the last day are those in whose hearts and lives God will have written his law, his Torah. As Paul will make clear later on in the letter, this process cannot be done by the Torah alone; God has now done in Christ and by the Spirit what the Torah wanted to do but could not do. So the question presses: who will these people be?

In 2:17-24 Paul declares that it cannot be the Jews as defined by race. Their racial boast – that national Israel is inalienably the people of God – is completely undercut by the continuance of Israel's exilic state. The existence of sin within Israel means that she cannot be affirmed as she stands. But supposing, says Paul in 2:25-29 – supposing there exist some true Jews, in whom the new covenant has been inaugurated? Supposing there are some in whom the new covenant promises of Jeremiah and Ezekiel are coming true? Whether they are racially Jews or not, whether they are circumcised or not, they will be regarded by God as his true covenant people. This is the doctrine of justification, or rather its first key move: there will come a time, a great day, on which God will vindicate his true people. But how can we know more precisely who they are?

More especially, how can God be true to the covenant if his covenant people, through whom he would redeem the world, have played him false? This is the question of 3:1-9. The key here is the verb 'entrusted' in verse 2: 'To begin with, the Jews were *entrusted* with the oracles of God'. God entrusted Israel with the message for the world; but if the messenger has proved unfaithful, does that mean the sender is faithless? Of course not. What is needed is a faithful messenger, a true Israelite, who will complete and accomplish the covenantal task: to deal finally with the sin of the world, the sin because of which not only Gentiles (as Jews believed) but also Jews (as the Torah made clear) stand in the dock, defenceless, before the creator (3:19f.). The Jewish longing for a great law-court scene, a great assize, in which they would be on one side and the Gentiles on the other, seems to have gone horribly wrong. But this prepares the way for Romans 3:21-31, in which God's solution to the problem is disclosed. God has now revealed his righteousness, his covenant faithfulness, through the faithfulness of the true Jew, the Messiah, Jesus of Nazareth.

Paul's theology as a Christian began with this realization: that what he had expected God to do for Israel at the end of all things, God had done for Jesus in the middle of all things. In and through Jesus Israel's hope had been realized. He had been raised from the dead, after suffering and dying at the hands of the pagans. This fact lies at the heart of the crucial paragraph 3:21-31.

[21] But now God's righteousness has been revealed apart from the law — though the law and the prophets bear witness to it: [22] it is God's righteousness, through the faithfulness of Jesus the Messiah, for all who believe. For there is no distinction: [23] for all sinned, and came short of the glory of God, [24] and they are justified freely, by his grace, through the redemption which is in the Messiah Jesus.

[25] God put him forth as a means of atonement, through faithfulness, by means of his blood; this was to demonstrate God's righteousness, because, in his forbearance, he had passed over previous sins. [26] It was to demonstrate his righteousness in the present time — that he himself might be in the right, and might justify people by Jesus' faithfulness.

[27] Where then is boasting? It is excluded. By what sort of law? The law of works? No, but through the law of faith. [28] For we reckon that a person is justified by faith, without works of the law. [29] Or is God the God of Jews only? Is he not of Gentiles also? Yes, of Gentiles also — [30] since God is one, and will justify the circumcised by faith and the uncircumcised through faith. [31] Do we then abolish the law through faith? Certainly not! On the contrary, we uphold the law.

This paragraph tends to be read *either* as though it simply expounded a law-court scheme of justification, with the bits about Jews and Gentiles as essentially an aside, *or* as though it were really all about the inclusion of Gentiles within the people of God, with the law-court material as a side-issue. Either way, the obviously covenantal material in verses 24-26, which we studied in the previous chapter, is regularly dismissed, perhaps a pre-Pauline fragment untidily included.

To approach the passage as I have done, however, sets up a context in which these false distinctions can be avoided. The passage is all about the covenant, membership in which is now thrown open to Jew and Gentile alike; *therefore* it is all about God's dealing with sin in the cross and resurrection of Jesus, because that was what the covenant was intended to do in the first place. The law court takes its proper place as the metaphorical means through which the covenant purposes of God are fulfilled. Once we fully grasp the nature of Pauline covenant theology, the fears that some have expressed, that a 'covenantal' reading of Paul will do away with a proper theology of sin and the cross, are shown to be groundless. The purpose of the covenant, which was to deal with the sin of the world, has been accomplished in the cross of Jesus Christ the Lord.

'Where then is boasting?' asks Paul in 3:27. 'It is excluded!' This 'boasting' which is excluded is not the boasting of the successful moralist; it is the racial boast of the Jew, as in 2:17-24. If this is not so, 3:29 ('Or is God the God of Jews only? Is he not of Gentiles also?') is a *non sequitur*. Paul has no thought in this passage of warding off a proto-Pelagianism, of which in any case his contemporaries were not guilty. He is here, as in Galatians and Philippians, declaring that there is no road into covenant membership on the grounds of Jewish racial privilege.

Within this context, 'justification', as seen in 3:24-26, means that those who believe in Jesus Christ are declared to be members of the true covenant family; which of course means that their sins are forgiven, since that was the purpose of the covenant. They are given the status of being 'righteous' in the metaphorical law court. When this is cashed out in terms of the underlying covenantal theme, it means that they are declared, in the present, to be what they will be seen to be in the future, namely the true people of God. Present justification declares, on the basis of faith, what future justification will affirm publicly (according to 2:14-16 and 8:9-11) on the basis of the entire life. And in making this declaration (3:26), God himself is in the right, in that he has been faithful to the covenant; he has dealt with sin, and upheld the helpless; and in the crucified Christ he has done so impartially. The gospel – not 'justification by faith', but the message about Jesus – thus reveals the righteousness, that is, the covenant faithfulness, of God.

What then about Romans 4? Romans 4, in which Paul discusses the faith of Abraham, is not, as is so often suggested, a detached 'proof from scripture' of an abstract doctrine. It is an exposition of the biblical covenant theology which has now been unveiled in the gospel. Genesis 15 is the backbone of the whole chapter – Genesis 15, that is, seen as the chapter in which the covenant with Abraham was established in the first place. When Paul speaks of Abraham's faith being 'reckoned as righteousness' (4:5), he means that faith in Jesus Christ – or, in Abraham's case, faith that God would give him a worldwide family despite his extreme age – is the true badge of covenant membership. Granted universal sinfulness, this means (once again) that faith of this sort is the badge of the sin-forgiven family. The emphasis of the chapter is therefore that covenant membership is defined, not by circumcision (4:9-12), nor by race, but by faith. That is why Abraham's family can be, and in Christ already is, a multi-ethnic family. Moreover, because of *what* is believed, the nature of faith itself is changed. If you believe in a distant and powerless god, the sort of faith you have will be dry and barren. If you believe in the God who raises the dead, your faith will be lively and life-giving. Abraham grew strong in faith (4:18-21) because he believed in this God, the God who raises the dead. This faith was not something Abraham 'did' in order to earn the right to be within the people of God. It was the badge which showed that he was a member – indeed, the founding member – of that people.

On this basis, Paul argues in Romans 5–8 that all who believe this gospel are the true, sin-forgiven, people of God, who are thus assured of their future salvation, which will consist in their resurrection as one aspect of the renewal of all of God's world. In 5:12-21 Paul stands back from the picture he has sketched and says, in effect: there you are – God's purpose in the covenant was to deal with the sin of Adam. Now, in Christ Jesus, that is exactly what he has done. The Torah could only offer slavery, since it accentuated the Jews' problem, namely, that they were 'in Adam'. The chosen people were as human, and fallen, as everyone else. But now (8:1-4) God has done what the Torah really wanted to do. He has given life to the world, life which will finally have the effect of liberating the entire cosmos, not just humans, from the effects of sin and death (8:18-27). It is this outworking of the gospel, and of justification, that is then celebrated in 8:31-39, where Paul returns to the eschatological, final justification which will consist in the resurrection of all Christ's people, their vindication after their suffering in the present time.

The other passage in Romans, finally, which deals with justification is such a clear example of the case I am arguing that I may perhaps be excused from spending much time on it. The passage from Romans 9:30 – 10:21 sets out the results of what God has done in Israel's history. God has called Israel to be the means of salvation for the world. His intention always was to narrow this vocation down to the Messiah, so that in his death all, Jew and Gentile alike, would find salvation. If, however, Israel insists on keeping her status for herself, she will find she is clinging to her own death-warrant.

Thus (to follow the train of thought from verse 9:30 onwards), while Gentiles are discovering covenant membership, characterized by faith, Israel, clinging to the Torah which defined covenant membership, did not attain to the Torah. She was determined to have her covenant membership demarcated by works of Torah, that is, by the things that kept that membership confined to Jews and Jews only; and, as a result, she did not submit to God's covenant purposes, his righteousness (10:3f.); for Christ is the end or goal of the law, so that all who believe may receive covenant membership. Christ has fulfilled the covenant purposes, bringing them to their God-ordained climax, which was always to deal with sin and so to set in motion the renewal of the whole cosmos. Now that purpose is fulfilled, what remains is mission (10:9ff.). So the letter to the Romans goes on its way: not as a detached statement of how people get saved, how they enter a relationship with God as individuals, but as an exposition of the covenant purposes of the creator God. The letter emphasizes above all the mission and unity of the church, as the things most necessary for the Romans to grasp if they are to be the base for the further westward expansion of Paul's mission.

Conclusion

Let me sum up Paul's doctrine of justification. We had better take this carefully, step by step, according to the three key categories I mentioned earlier, namely, the covenant, the law court, and eschatology.

1. Covenant. Justification is the covenant declaration, which will be issued on the last day, in which the true people of God will be vindicated and those who insist on worshipping false gods will be shown to be in the wrong.

2. Law court. Justification functions like the verdict in the law court: by acquitting someone, it confers on that person the status 'righteous'. This is the forensic dimension of the future *covenantal* vindication.

3. Eschatology. This declaration, this verdict, is ultimately to be made at the end of history. Through Jesus, however, God has done in the middle of history what he had been expected to do — and, indeed, will still do — at the end; so that the declaration, the verdict, can be issued already in the present, in anticipation. The events of the last days were *anticipated* when Jesus died on the cross, as the representative Messiah of Israel, and rose again. (This was Paul's own theological starting-point.) The verdict of the last day is therefore now also anticipated in the present, whenever someone believes in the gospel message about Jesus.

4. Therefore — and this is the vital thrust of the argument of Galatians in particular, but it plays a central role in Philippians and Romans as well — all who believe the gospel of Jesus Christ are already demarcated as members of the true family of Abraham, with their sins being forgiven.

They are demarcated by their faith – specifically, by their believing of the 'gospel' message of the sovereignty of Jesus Christ. This is the meaning of the crucial term, 'justification apart from works of the law'. The badges of membership by which some Jews had sought to demarcate themselves in the present time, ahead of the eschatological verdict, were focused upon the works of the law – the works, that is, which marked them out as covenant-keepers, as true Israel. The 'works of the law' – sabbath, food-laws, circumcision – thus enabled them to attain a measure of what scholars have called 'inaugurated eschatology', the anticipation in the present of what is to come in the future. The verdict of the future (God's vindication of his true Israel over the rest of the world) was anticipated in the present, in Jesus Christ.

Paul, as usual, retains the *shape* of the Jewish doctrine, while filling it with new *content*. For him, covenant membership was defined by the gospel itself, that is, by Jesus Christ. The badge of membership, the thing because of which one can tell *in the present* who is within the *eschatological* covenant people, was of course faith, the confession that Jesus is Lord and the belief that God raised him from the dead (Romans 10:9). 'Faith', for Paul, is therefore not a substitute 'work' in a moralistic sense. It is not something one does in order to gain admittance into the covenant people. It is the badge that proclaims that one is already a member. Likewise, 'faith' for Paul is not a general religious awareness, or a general romantic opposition to moralism and preference for a religion of inward feeling. It is very precise and specific. It is faith in the gospel message, the announcement of the true God as defined in and through Jesus Christ.

Two conclusions to this discussion suggest themselves, in relation to some current discussions of the subject.

First, it becomes apparent that Sanders has not carried his reform far enough; but that, when it is carried as far as it should be, it turns out not to undermine, but rather to flesh out more fully, a thoroughly orthodox reading of Paul. The false antitheses of Wrede, Schweitzer, Bultmann, Davies, Käsemann, Sanders and many others, by which Paul has been dismembered in the search for coherence, must be put aside. A covenantal reading of Paul, such as I have suggested, holds together the otherwise disparate elements of his thought, allowing each aspect, not least Christology and the cross, to appear more clearly, not less, than before.

Second, I must stress again that the doctrine of justification by faith is not what Paul means by 'the gospel'. It is *implied* by the gospel; when the gospel is proclaimed, people come to faith and so are regarded by God as members of his people. But 'the gospel' is not an account of how people get saved. It is, as we saw in an earlier chapter, the proclamation of the lordship of Jesus Christ. If we could only get that clear in current debates, a lot of other false antitheses, not least in thinking about the mission of the church, would quietly unravel before our eyes. Let us be quite clear. 'The gospel' is the announcement of Jesus' lordship, which works with power to bring people into the family of Abraham, now redefined around Jesus Christ and characterized solely by faith in him. 'Justification' is the doctrine which insists that all those who have this faith belong as full members of this family, on this basis and no other.

The thumbnail sketch I have given of several aspects of Paul's gospel and theology thus points quite directly to the question: what is the effect of this gospel, and this doctrine, in terms of the actual life of actual people? The next two chapters address this, first in terms of Paul's own contemporaries and then in terms of today.

Notes

1. Alister McGrath, *Iustitia Dei. A History of the Christian Doctrine of Justification,* 1986, volume 1, page 2 and following.
2. Alister McGrath, *Iustitia Dei*, 1986, volume 1, page 1.

CH 5-7 The Good News for the nations and for Israel is Jesus, but his significance is revealed to them in unique ways

CHAPTER 8

God's Renewed Humanity

So far in this book I have attempted to set out a view of Paul, his work and his thought in terms of the way in which the Jewish agenda and theology of Saul of Tarsus was radically rethought, but not essentially abandoned, in the Christian agenda and theology of Paul the apostle. He was still 'zealous', but claimed that his zeal was now 'according to knowledge', the knowledge of the one true God which he had discovered in the face of the crucified and risen Jesus. He still had a polemical engagement with the pagans, but he now also had good news for them. He was still critical of his fellow-Jews, but now for a different reason. He had good news for them, too, news of how the God whom they worshipped had unveiled the shocking secret plan he had been preparing all along.

We have seen that Paul claimed the high ground over against paganism, setting out a vision of the true God, the world, and of human life which offered itself as the reality of which paganism is the parody. At the same time, his critique of Judaism was not that Judaism was a bad thing, but that it had – apart from its Messiah – failed in the task for which it had been created. He developed, in short, what he saw as a truly Jewish theology and mission, which was precisely the means of bringing to the pagan world the truth, and the true way of life, for which it dimly groped but which it could not attain. The zeal of Saul of Tarsus was thus transformed into the zeal of Paul the apostle; and, because this specific transformation involved the recognition, at its very heart, that the God of Israel was now revealed in and as the crucified and risen Jesus of Nazareth, Israel's Messiah, Paul's 'zeal' itself radically changed in character. No longer was it violent, aimed at winning God's battles by brute force. It lost none of its energy; but that energy was now characterized by the thing that Paul saw at the very heart of the God he learnt to worship afresh: the quality which he called *agape* – love.

135

This way of looking at the transition from Saul to Paul offers, I believe, several new possibilities for understanding and applying what he said. In this chapter I want to concentrate on one in particular, namely, Paul's vision of God's renewed humanity. What Paul said about the renewal of humanity in Christ belongs exactly on the map I have drawn. On the one hand, he believed that humanity renewed in Christ was the genuine article, explicitly contrasted with the fractured and downgraded humanity which characterized paganism. On the other hand, he believed that humanity renewed in Christ was the fulfilment of the vocation of Israel, which unbelieving Israel was failing to attain. Paul was now zealous to promote this genuine humanity as the God-given answer to paganism, and to urge Jews who were missing out on it that this was in fact the true fulfilment of their history and tradition.

Paul articulated, in other words, *a way of being human* which he saw as the true way. In his ethical teaching, in his community development, and above all in his theology and practice of new life through dying and rising with Christ, he zealously articulated, modelled, inculcated, and urged upon his converts a way of life which he saw as being the genuinely human way of life. And he saw this as the way of life to which Judaism had been called, but to which, without the Messiah, Judaism had not attained and could not attain. I shall try to show, then, that Paul's vision of the renewal of humanity in Christ is not simply a one-dimensional ethic. It is not simply a matter of 'getting saved' and then 'learning how to behave'. It is a multi-textured vision, woven together to meet various specific needs, and promoted with all the energy that, Paul declared, his God had inspired within him.

The Centre of Renewed Humanity: Worship

The first category chooses itself. At the centre of Paul's vision of genuine humanity is the true worship of the one true God. Over against the pagan worship of idols, and as the fulfilment of the Jewish goal of offering true worship to the true God, Paul places the worship of the God now revealed in Jesus the Messiah, and in the Spirit of Jesus, the Holy Spirit.

We meet this at the beginning of one of his earliest letters. In 1 Thessalonians 1:9 he describes what happened when he first preached the gospel to the Thessalonians. 'You turned', he says, 'from idols, to worship the living and true God, and to wait for his Son from heaven, whom he raised from the dead, Jesus, who delivers us from the wrath to come.' This not only serves, of course, as an introduction to the letter; it points us to the basic thing that Paul looked for when he preached the gospel to pagans. He saw the pagan world as characterized by idolatry. He longed to see this replaced with worship of the true God.

To see the contrast spelled out a little, we return to two passages we examined earlier in a different context (see chapter 3, 'The Gospel of God'). First, we must look at Galatians 4:1-11. This is part of his argument that the Galatian Christians, having believed in Christ and been filled with the Spirit, do not need in addition to become physical members of Judaism. In this context, and as part of the argument, he sets out his basic view of God: the one who sent the Son, the one who sends the Spirit of the Son. Then at once he asks: 'How, when you have come to know God, or rather to be known by God, can you turn back again to pagan idols?'

Here we see the double-edged thrust of Paul's call to true worship. He presupposes that this true worship, of the God known as the Father of the Son and the sender of the Spirit, is the truth, the reality, of which pagan idolatry is the parody. But, to our surprise and perhaps our horror, we discover that from this perspective unbelieving Judaism itself stands revealed as *a compromise with paganism*. Adherence to Torah, in the way that Paul's opponents are advocating it, is no better than pagan idolatry. To undergo circumcision is, in effect, to give in to the principalities and powers. It is to step back into a scheme of blood, soil, race and tribe. It is like going back to the paganism renounced at conversion.

The reason for this remarkable polemical twist in the argument will become clear later on. But, first, let us observe the same phenomenon in our second passage: 1 Corinthians 8:1-6. Here, once again, Paul is claiming the high ground over against paganism. We, he says, are worshippers of the one true God. That is our basic stance, when confronted with questions about how to live within a pagan society (the specific question at issue here being the eating of meat that had been offered to idols). And, as the proof of his point, and to set the foundations for his subsequent argument, he quotes the Jewish confession of faith, the basic element of Jewish prayer and worship, namely the *Shema*: Hear, O Israel, the Lord our God, the Lord is one. But, as we saw in chapter 4, he *rewrites* the *Shema*, putting Jesus within it: for us, he says, there is one God – the Father, from whom are all things and we to him – and one Lord, Jesus Christ, through whom are all things and we through him. At the heart of the Jewish confession of faith there now stands the Jewish Messiah. Paul is claiming the high ground, the Jewish ground, the worship of the true God over against pagan idolatry. But when we examine that high Jewish worship of the one God it turns out to contain a challenge to the Judaism that cannot or will not recognize its God in the face of Jesus. The one true God is now known, for Paul, as the Father of Jesus the Messiah.

Once we see this point, we may be able to recognize the same theology when we meet it expanded into a whole argument. The whole point of the long paragraph which begins in Romans 1:18 is that Gentiles are idolaters, and that therefore their humanity self-destructs. Idolatry, Paul is saying, is seriously bad for the health of your humanity. The pagan world knows God, because in creation pagans can see his eternal power and deity; but they refuse to honour him as God or worship him, and turn instead to worship images of birds, animals and reptiles. As a result (since humans become like what they worship: this is a basic spiritual law), they cease to exhibit true and full humanity, reflecting the image of God. They exhibit, instead, all the signs of a humanity that is coming apart at the seams:

> They are filled with all injustice, wickedness, covetousness, evil. Full of envy, murder, jealousy, trickery, craftiness, they are plotters, slanderers, God-haters, arrogant, proud, boastful, inventors of evil, rebellious towards parents, foolish, faithless, heartless, ruthless. (Romans 1:29-31)

Paul is here following through the lines of a typical Jewish critique of the pagan world. The normal Jewish response would be to say: well, but we are the people of God, who know God, who worship him truly, who have been set up as the light of the nations. Paul anticipates this in 2:17-24: the Jewish boast cannot be made good, because *Israel is still in exile*, still under the curse which shows that she shares at a deep level the problem of the rest of humanity. Instead of bringing the Gentiles to worship God, the prophets charged Israel with bringing God's name into disrepute (2:24, quoting Isaiah 52:5).

What then is the solution? God has called into being a new community (2:25-29), in which circumcision and uncircumcision are alike irrelevant, and in which what matters is whether or not one is – a Jew! Paul does not even say 'a *true* Jew'; his point, in 2:29, is sharp and should not be blunted.

The only person who truly deserves the name 'Jew', he says, is the one who is so in secret, in the heart, in the spirit not in the letter; that person's praise is not from other humans, but from God. There is, then, a people that worships God in truth. This people is the true humanity, the people that Israel was supposed to be but had failed to be. Paul will zealously announce this one true God, and summon people to worship him, knowing that in so doing he is confronting pagan idolatry on the one hand and fulfilling the destiny of Israel on the other.

This is not the last word on the subject in Romans, by a long way. We might note, particularly, the way in which the picture of Abraham and his faith in Romans 4 explicitly reverses the picture of Adamic humanity and its idolatry in Romans 1. In 1:20-23 Paul describes how humanity as a whole knows God but fails to worship him:

> God's eternal power and deity are clearly perceived, so that they are without excuse: though they knew God, did not give him glory as God, or thank him, but became foolish in their reasonings, and their senseless mind was darkened. Claiming to be wise, they became fools...

In Romans 4:19-21, by contrast, Paul describes how Abraham

> did not grow weak in faith as he considered his own body, which was as good as dead... he did not waver in unbelief before the promise of God, but grew strong in faith, giving glory to God, fully convinced that he was able to perform that which he had promised.

Pagan, Adamic humanity looked at God's power and deity and instead worshipped elements of the world. Abraham looked at the deadly reality of the world – specifically, his own and Sarah's bodies, as good as dead because of age – and refused to let his horizon be determined by that. Instead, he gave God the glory and trusted him to fulfil his promises. We are rightly told by the commentators that Abraham's faith is the subject of Romans 4; but it is not so often noticed that the centre of that faith is the worship of the one true God. And that, Paul claims, not only challenges pagan idolatry; it characterizes all those who believe that God raised Jesus from the dead. In other words, worship of this sort, though it is of course the truly Jewish worship, marks out the Christian community over against unbelieving Judaism. The end of this train of thought comes when, following a great Jewish-style paean of praise to the God whose ways are unsearchable and incomprehensible (11:33-36), Paul takes a deep breath and summons his readers to the worship of this God, and the human transformation that results. I shall return to this presently. Being grasped by the gospel as Paul has expounded it, in other words, means worshipping the true God, and so reflecting this God *by becoming a more complete human being*. Genuine humanness resulting from true worship: that is Paul's vision.

The Goal of Renewed Humanity: Resurrection

If the road to true humanity is true worship, the end and goal of God's renewed humanity is of course resurrection. To set this topic out in full would be too complex for the present book, and I shall shorten and simplify it as best I can. The fundamental texts, for those who wish to pursue the matter further, are 1 Corinthians 15; Romans 8; Colossians 3; 2 Corinthians 4 and 5; and the closing verses of Philippians 3.

The basic point I wish to make can be stated as follows. When Paul is expounding the resurrection hope of God's people in Christ he is again offering a reality of which (in his view) paganism is the parody; and, again, announcing the reality to which Judaism had pointed. Paganism was pretty unclear about just what it could hope for in the hereafter. There was a range of speculation on the topic, with all sorts of dreams of immortality, and hopes of this or that sort of a life beyond the grave. One way to understand what Paul is doing, not least in the Corinthian letters, is to see him as taking on paganism and attempting to defeat it on its own terms. The hope of resurrection – not, as he says, to be unclothed, but to be more fully clothed – is the reality of the future life; paganism offers mere parodies of it. Resurrection is not simply resuscitation; it is transformation, the changing of the present mode of physicality into a new mode, of which Jesus in his risen body is the only prototype, but for which the transformation of a seed into a plant can function as a general analogy. This is the creator's plan for the future of his human creatures.

In his doctrine of resurrection, Paul avoids two opposite dangers: the divinization of the created order and the dualistic rejection of the created order. Stoicism, being basically pantheist, saw the material world as basically divine. But in that case, there could never be any real change in the world;

history would go on repeating itself, dissolving into fire at the end of the present age and then starting up all over again with the identical events happening all over again. Paul's doctrine of resurrection, standing firmly on the Jewish view of God, the world and history, offered a positive evaluation of the created order – since the creator would reaffirm it by transforming it into the reality of which at the moment it was only the seed – without for a moment suggesting that the material world was itself divine. 'God gives it a body'; there, in 1 Corinthians 15:38, we have the basic answer to pagan views of life after death.

But once more, at the same time, Paul's exposition of resurrection offers a clear alternative to the Jewish beliefs current in his day, so far as we can grasp them (there is more variety, and complexity, than is at times supposed). Resurrection, for Saul of Tarsus as a Shammaite Pharisee, was bound up with the national hope of Israel. Israel would be raised to life, while the Gentiles received their punishment. What is more, the hope was sometimes expressed in terms that were more like a resuscitation: God would restore Israel back into the present world. Over against this, Paul offers in 1 Corinthians 15 a kind of Christianized apocalypse: no longer are the Gentiles the real enemy, but instead sin and death themselves are the enemies that God will destroy in the last great act of the drama.

What is more, because of the death and resurrection of Jesus Paul sees that the Christian answer to the question 'What time is it?' is radically different from the Jewish answer. As a Pharisee he would have answered: we are living in the last days before the great act of God within history to defeat the pagans and liberate Israel. As a Christian he answered: we are living in the first days after the great act of God within history to defeat sin and death and liberate the whole cosmos. He would then have added: these are also the last days before the great act of God which will bring to completion that which was begun in Christ. But the first statement is the more important; and it is this which offers not only a critique of paganism, in its view of what will happen to humanity after death, but also a critique of unbelieving Judaism. Paul's view of the goal of renewed humanity, then, is that God's renewed humans will share a resurrection like that of Jesus Christ; and this vision of the goal offers the reality of which paganism is the parody, and the reality towards which Judaism had strained but which it had not finally attained.

A footnote is necessary at this point. It is often assumed that Paul's horizon was dominated by the expectation that the space-time universe was about to come to an end. The apocalyptic passage in 1 Thessalonians, and the warning about the present time being 'constrained' in 1 Corinthians 7:29-31, have been pressed into service to suggest that Paul believed something which, as I have argued in detail elsewhere, neither first-century Jews at large nor Jesus and the earliest Christians in particular believed.[1] The twentieth-century world of New Testament scholarship, not least those parts that have inveighed against 'literalism' of the fundamentalist sort, has all too often insisted on a literal reading of that regular Jewish language – the sun and the moon being darkened, and so forth – which, from its biblical context, we ought to know was intended, and understood, as powerful metaphor.

Paul expected great, cataclysmic events; there is no doubt of that. He was urgent about his work, knowing there were things to be done before those events happened. He also believed that at some stage in the future the God who had made the entire cosmos would 'set it free from its bondage to decay' (Romans 8:21). At the end, God would be 'all in all', having subjugated all rival powers (1 Corinthians 15:23-28). But we should not too quickly confuse this larger horizon of expectation with the immediate crisis that Paul knows is about to break upon the world. Jews of his day, as of other days, were used to 'seeing' space-time, political events in terms of 'the Day of the Lord'. Otherwise, why would he tell the Thessalonians not to worry if they received a letter, supposedly from him, saying that the Day of the Lord had already arrived (2 Thessalonians 2:2)? If 'the Day of the Lord' meant the end of the space-time universe, one might suppose that the Thessalonians would not need to be informed of this event by mail. We have for too long allowed ourselves to be boxed in, in our reading of Paul, by the end-of-the-world agenda. It is time to see Paul as he understood himself: as someone living already in the beginning of God's new age, the age which began on Easter morning.

The Transformation of Renewed Humanity: Holiness

What happens in between the beginning and the end of this renewed humanity? What happens, that is, between the moment when pagans, and indeed Jews, come to worship the true God revealed in Jesus Christ, and the moment when they find themselves transformed in the life of the resurrection? Paul's basic answer is that the transformation begins in the here and now. The classic text is of course Romans 12:1-2:

> I appeal to you, brothers and sisters, through the mercy of God, to present your bodies as a living sacrifice, holy, acceptable to God: this is your true and appropriate worship. Do not be conformed to the present age, but be transformed by the renewal of your mind, so that you may approve the will of God, that which is good, acceptable, and complete.

Here we have it all in a nutshell: worship and holiness joined together. Again, Romans 1:18-32 is explicitly reversed. The mind and the body are both fully engaged; indeed, what Paul is offering here is a *re-integrated* humanity, over against the disintegration which is the hallmark of Adamic humanity, pagan humanity, in Romans 1.

This time it is not difficult to see the way in which his vision is the explicit alternative to paganism. 'Do not be conformed to this world, but be transformed'; in other words, don't let the pagan world shape your worldview, your praxis, your symbolic universe, your thinking, your narratival world. Paganism is a self-destructive mode of being human; Paul offers, instead, the fulfilment of the Jewish vision of humanity, a humanity characterized by wisdom and holiness.

Holiness is a complex and difficult topic. I simply want to stress, under this heading, that Paul sees holiness not as an optional extra, not as something to which some Christians are called while others are allowed to stay in a state of semi-paganism, but as something which necessarily characterizes all those who are renewed in Christ. At the same time, he is a realist. He does not suppose, as some commentators have assumed he supposes, that Christians are able, in virtue of their baptism, the indwelling of the Spirit, or whatever, to live a hundred-per-cent holy life all the time. He faces the problems that arise from this apparent tension, and deals with them. That is what a letter like 1 Corinthians is all about. For him, the life of the renewed humanity is held in the tension of the 'now' and the 'not yet', always called to worship the true God and so to be renewed day by day in the image of the creator (Colossians 3), and at the same time always looking ahead eagerly to what is yet to come. 'I do not think that I have already attained it; but one thing I do, forgetting what lies behind and straining forward for what lies ahead, I press on towards the goal for the prize of the upward call of God in Christ Jesus' (Philippians 3:12-14).

143

In particular, Paul does not think that holiness is to be had by following the Jewish Torah in the way that, as a Pharisee, he had done so zealously, and indeed had insisted upon for others. Inbuilt into his exposition of Christian holiness is the strong critique of Torah: it is simply incapable of giving the holy life it holds out. The crucial passages here are Romans 7 and Galatians 5, both highly controversial in exegetical debate.

In both Romans 7 and Galatians 5, I suggest, Paul describes Israel as being in the flesh, in Adam, so that when Israel embraces Torah all it can do is condemn her. We take Romans 7 first; here Paul uses the autobiographical device, the 'I', not least to avoid giving the appearance of criticizing his fellow-Jews as though from a distance. The plight he describes is that which, from his Christian standpoint, he realizes he had been in as a zealous Pharisee. Israel, he suggests, is right to embrace Torah, because it is indeed holy, and just, and good. It does indeed point to the goal of true humanity. But because Israel is still in Adam, the holy just and good law must condemn her. It can do no other. 'That which promised life proved to be death to me.' Only when the basic condition of Israel's Adamic humanness has been dealt with in Christ – which happens, for Paul, in the death and resurrection of Jesus, and in the Christian identification with those events in baptism – can 'the law of the Spirit of life set you free from the law of sin and death' (Romans 8:2).

In Galatians 5, Paul faces the fact that the Galatians are eager to embrace Torah, not least because they want to move as far away from their old pagan lifestyle as they possibly can. They have seen their former pagan idolatry and immorality for what they are, and are determined to go instead for the way of true humanity, of holiness and worship. The 'agitators' (those who infiltrated the Galatian community after Paul had left) have told them that they can achieve this end by embracing Torah. Not so, says Paul: if you do that you will simply be emphasizing that which binds you to the old humanity, to the flesh. The fact that the sign of embracing Torah is circumcision makes this point even more sharply. If you take on Torah, you won't be raising yourself to a height above that of your former pagan life, above even that of your new Christian (but not Torah-observant) life; you will be reducing yourself once more to the level of paganism, emphasizing the flesh, that which binds you to the old humanity. As a result, you will again be in the self-destructive mode of human existence. If you want the genuine article, you must walk by the Spirit, whose fruit is love, joy and peace.

Throughout Paul's writings, genuine holiness is seen in terms of dying and rising with Christ. This theme is never more clearly expressed than in 2 Corinthians, where Paul, writing out of great pain and grief, grapples with a community that has failed to grasp the significance of the gospel in terms of its own life, and that in consequence has rejected him and his style of apostleship. They don't want a suffering jailbird of a leader; they want someone with power and prestige, someone they can look up to. In a letter full of brilliant rhetoric and personal revelation, Paul demonstrates both in what he says and how he says it that the cross and resurrection of Jesus the Messiah really are the centre and driving force of the life of the renewed humanity.

> As servants of God we have commended ourselves in every way: through great endurance, in afflictions, hardships, calamities, beatings, imprisonments, riots, labours, sleepless nights, hunger; by purity, knowledge, patience, kindness, holiness of spirit, genuine love, truthful speech, and the power of God; with the weapons of righteousness for the right hand and the left; in honour and dishonour, in ill repute and good repute. We are treated as impostors, and yet are true; as unknown, and yet are well known; as dying, and see – we are alive; as punished, and yet not killed; as sorrowful, yet always rejoicing; as poor, yet making many rich; as having nothing, and yet possessing everything. (2 Corinthians 6:4-10)

The death and resurrection of Jesus the Messiah are not, for Paul, merely events in the past, however climactic. They are the foundation of his, and the church's, daily existence. 'Sharing the sufferings of Christ, in order to share his glory also'; that is the keynote of what Paul means by holiness. Genuine humanness does not come cheap.

This leads us, none too soon, to the fifth category of the renewed humanity.

The Coherence of
Renewed Humanity: Love

We have already seen that Paul analyzes the world of paganism in terms of the fracturing of genuine humanity. This occurs, as we find it in Romans 1, even within the individual human being. But it occurs also, devastatingly, when one category of human beings define themselves against another. For Paul, this is not just the activity of human beings in their pride and fear, though of course it is that as well. It is the result of the work of the principalities and powers, carving up the world between them; of the *stoicheia*, the 'elements', the local or tribal deities that were believed to govern the different nations. And, for Paul, these are, all of them, defeated in Christ. That is why there is now neither Jew nor Greek, slave nor free, no male and female, but all are one in Christ Jesus (Galatians 3:28). At this point, therefore, the central characteristic of the renewed humanity is love.

A brief word about love. Paul does not mean that all Christians should feel warm fuzzy feelings for each other. That romantic and existentialist reading of *agape* does not begin to capture what is really going on. The critical thing is that the church, those who worship God in Christ Jesus, should function as a family in which every member is accepted as an equal member, no matter what their social, cultural or moral background. The very existence of such a community demonstrates to the principalities and powers, the hidden but powerful forces of prejudice and suspicion, that their time is up, that the living God has indeed won the victory over them, that there is now launched upon the world a different way of being human, a way in which the traditional distinctions between human beings are done away with. That is why we find in Ephesians the climactic statement: the purpose of the gospel is that 'through the church the manifold wisdom of God might be made known to the principalities and powers in the heavenly places' (Ephesians 3:10). The very existence of a community of love, love where before there was mutual suspicion and distrust, is the crucial piece of evidence that tells Paul that God's spirit has been at work (Colossians 1:8).

Clearly, the existence and flourishing of such a community is the thing that is going to reveal to the pagan world that the gospel of Jesus Christ is what it claims to be. That is why, when writing 1 Corinthians, Paul builds up his argument step by step, showing at point after point the way in which this community is radically different from its pagan neighbours, until at last he reaches chapter 13, when, like the chorale theme in Sibelius' 'Finlandia', the clear poetry in praise of love, *agape*, rings out, and we realize that this was all along the subtext of the entire letter:

Love is patient and kind;
Love is not jealous or boastful,
It is not arrogant or rude;
Love does not seek its own ends,
It is not irritable, keeps no record of wrongs,
Does not rejoice over injustice,
But celebrates the truth;
Love bears all things
Believes all things,
Hopes all things,
Endures all things...

So now there remain faith, hope, love, these three;
But the greatest of these is love.

Everything Paul has said so far on every topic has been, after all, an appeal for *agape*. This is the lifestyle that reveals what genuine renewed humanity is all about. Paganism is always trying to ape it, but all it can do is collapse into personality cults, factional fighting (it's very easy, after all, to 'love' everyone else in your faction; that's the point of having a faction in the first place), and blatant eroticism, which parodies the life of *agape* at the same time as it progressively distorts, defaces, and destroys the human beings who live in that way.

Once again, though, this life of *agape* serves also as a critique from within of the Pharisaic Judaism in which Paul had grown up. Notoriously and obviously, his appeal for the Jew-plus-Gentile united family in Christ cuts against all attempts to make Christianity a sub-branch of Judaism. Here we find some of his sharpest polemic; this, indeed, is why it is so sharp at precisely this point. He sees all too clearly that if the church splits into Jewish Christian and Gentile Christian factions, perhaps with some Gentile Christians joining the Jewish Christians by undergoing circumcision, this will mean that the principalities and powers are still after all ruling the world; that they have not after all been defeated by Christ on the cross; that there is no such thing as a renewed humanity, and that he has all along been whistling in the dark in pretending that there is.

The way he argues this point is, once again, to claim the highest of high ground. In Romans 4, and in Galatians 3 and 4, he argues that the coming into being of this Jew-plus-Gentile family of faith was what the one true God always had in mind, from the moment when he called Abraham. This was what the promises always envisaged. The fulfilment of God's purpose for Israel is (paradoxically from one point of view) precisely the transcending of the boundaries of Israel by the new, renewed humanity from every nation and tribe and tongue. The paradox is only apparent. As Paul expounds it again and again, the call of Israel, the purpose of election, always was, as far as God was concerned, undertaken for the salvation of the whole world. That is why the cross was the climactic moment of the covenant purpose of God. And that is why, in the creation of the renewed family in which traditional distinctions are transcended, Paul sees that paganism's parody of community is confronted with the reality, and that Judaism's distortion of that community receives its decisive critique from within its own tradition. Paul wrestles mightily with the fact that the communities he has founded by no means find it easy to live up to the vocation he has offered them. But that this is his vision there should be no doubt.

The Zeal of
Renewed Humanity: Mission

We saw in an earlier chapter that, for Paul, the lordship of Jesus Christ challenged the lordship of Caesar. This deserves (were there more space) to be explored in terms of the theology of power which grows out of the cross and resurrection, and which challenges and subverts the nature of power as we see it in paganism, especially in pagan empire. What I want to do here, however, is to draw attention to the way in which, through worshipping the one true God, Paul believes that the renewed humanity is set (strangely and paradoxically) in authority over the world. The mission of the church is the reality of which the pagan empire is the parody.

This has to do with Paul's underlying theology of the image of God restored in those who worship him truly. Christians, he says, are being 'renewed in knowledge after the image of the creator' (Colossians 3:10). They are chosen so as to be 'conformed to the image of the Son, so that he might be the firstborn among many brothers and sisters' (Romans 8:29). But what does it mean to think of humans being remade in God's image?

The doctrine of the image of God in his human creatures was never the belief simply that humans were meant to reflect God back to God. They were meant to reflect God out into the world. In Romans 8, therefore, we see quite clearly what the end of this process will be: when God's people are finally renewed completely, in the resurrection, then the whole creation will itself be set free from its bondage to decay, and share the glorious freedom of God's children. In the meantime, the mission of the church means announcing God's kingdom in all the world. Paul went about (according to Acts 17:7) saying that there was 'another king, namely Jesus'. He expects his followers to do the same.

Of course, Jesus is a different sort of king to Caesar. That is part of the point. Paul is not simply setting up a new empire of the same variety, another oppressive human regime. But it will not do to suppose that the differences between Christ and Caesar, for Paul, are that the one is 'spiritual' and the other 'temporal', so that they become locked in two separate compartments with no relation between them. The whole point of 'confessing Jesus Christ as Lord' is that at his name every knee shall bow. Caesar has a role (Romans 13), but a strictly limited one. He is to be obeyed because his office and authority are derived from the creator, who intends his human creatures to live in order, safety and stability, rather than in chaos or anarchy. As soon as Caesar acts as though he were a god — as of course in Paul's day most Caesars did — Paul would be the first to call a spade a spade. If the early Christian community saw the death of Herod Agrippa as divine judgment on a monarch who gave himself divine honours (Acts 12:20-23), there is no doubt what Paul would have said about pagan worship of the Roman emperor. There was only one God; this God had exalted his Son, Jesus, as the true Lord of the world; his empire was the reality, Caesar's the parody.

Paul's mission should not be thought of, then, merely in terms of individualistic evangelism, rescuing souls one by one for a future heaven. To be sure, in announcing the gospel of Jesus Christ as Lord he challenged every single hearer to submit in obedient faith to the lordship of Jesus Christ. To those who believed he gave the assurance that, as true members of the one family of God, they would be vindicated, raised from the dead, to share the glory of the new creation that was yet to come. But Paul did not see his mission merely in those terms. He speaks of the gospel being 'announced to every creature under heaven' (Colossians 1:23); he knows that what he is doing is simply part of a cosmic movement, beginning with the resurrection of Jesus and ending with the renewal of all things. He is, as we saw several chapters ago, the herald of the king; and the king is King of kings and Lord of lords. The Jewish hope, that Israel's king would be king of the world, had come true in Jesus the Messiah.

149

Conclusion

I have tried to show, throughout this book, how it was that the zeal of Saul of Tarsus was transformed into the zeal of Paul the apostle. I have argued that the basic shape of this zeal remained much the same: it was an energetic confrontation with paganism, and an equally energetic critique of compromised Judaism. The shape, however, was filled with new content, as Paul reworked the entire scheme around the death and resurrection of Jesus and the gift of the Spirit. What I have tried to show in this chapter, all too briefly, is that Paul held out to his hearers, urged upon his converts, and did his best to maintain in his churches, the reality of God's renewed humanity, which at every level and in every way proved to be the reality of which paganism was the parody, and at every level and in every way proved to be the fulfilment of Israel's aspirations, leaving unbelieving Israel revealed as deeply, though paradoxically, compromised with paganism. This vision of renewed humanity offers us a great deal of food for thought, not only at the academic level of understanding what Paul really said, but also within the life and mission of the church. It is to that topic that we turn in the next chapter.

Notes

1. See particularly *The New Testament and the People of God*, chapters 10 and 15; *Jesus and the Victory of God*, chapters 6 and 8.

CHAPTER 9

Paul's Gospel Then and Now

What I have said so far about what St Paul really said should be enough, I hope, to stimulate a fair amount of fresh thought about his meaning for today. But I want, at this point, to indicate some areas that I think need special highlighting. I have concentrated particularly in this book on two things: 'the gospel' and 'justification'.

For Paul, 'the gospel' creates the church; 'justification' defines it. The gospel announcement carries its own power to save people, and to dethrone the idols to which they had been bound. 'The gospel' itself is neither a system of thought, nor a set of techniques for making people Christians; it is the personal announcement of the person of Jesus. That is why it creates the church, the people who believe that Jesus is Lord and that God raised him from the dead. 'Justification' is then the doctrine which declares that whoever believes that gospel, and wherever and whenever they believe it, those people are truly members of his family, no matter where they came from, what colour their skin may be, whatever else might distinguish them from each other. The gospel itself creates the church; justification continually reminds the church that it is the people created by the gospel and the gospel alone, and that it must live on that basis.

On Thinking Paul's Thoughts

To begin with, I want to point out the way in which the sketch I have offered makes sense of what otherwise appear as puzzling antinomies or even contradictions at the heart of Paul's thought. I wrote in the first chapter

151

about the line of thought from Schweitzer to Sanders, which plays off 'law-court' terminology against what Schweitzer calls 'mystical' and Sanders calls 'participationist' categories. Once we grasp the covenantal nature of Paul's thought, and the way in which the covenant always carried the sense of God's great law court at its heart, this antinomy is revealed for what it is: a projection back on to Paul of a distinction which owes its origin to a much later philosophy and theology, and has little or nothing to do with the real Paul. For him, 'being in Christ' – the fundamental 'participationist' idea – means 'belonging to the people of God as redefined around the Messiah'. It is, in other words, a specifically *covenantal* way of speaking. Equally, however, the language of 'righteousness' – of God's own covenant faithfulness on the one hand, and of the status of covenant membership which God's people are given on the other, and the way in which both of these are seen through the metaphorical lens of the law court – is covenantal through and through. This is, I dare say, of enormous importance for those who, as part of their own preaching of Paul today, struggle with commentaries and books on Paul in which these categories are wrongly played off against one another.

The same is true for another debate which I haven't mentioned in this book so far, but which dominates some current American Pauline scholarship in particular, and likewise finds its way into commentaries and monographs. In reaction against some versions of a 'covenantal' reading of Paul, some scholars (such as J.L. Martyn) have emphasized the 'apocalyptic' nature of his thought. Covenantal categories, it is thought, imply a steady development from Abraham to Christ and beyond, with great continuity between Old and New Testament, between promise and fulfilment. What we find in Paul, however, is rather the (supposedly) 'apocalyptic' notion of a clean break, the rude shock of the crucifixion cutting across all previous expectation. 2 Corinthians 5:16 might function as a slogan for this: 'The old has passed away; behold, all things have become new'.

The problem, of course, is that that passage itself is fundamentally and explicitly covenantal. It is part of the great argument (2 Corinthians 3–6) about how the covenantal ministry of the apostle works itself out. That is symptomatic, I suggest, of the false antithesis which Martyn and others have set up. When we understand how Paul's covenantal categories work out, we see that they have the cross and resurrection at their heart. The one saving (covenantal) plan always was, so to speak, cruciform. The covenant was set up to deal with evil and death; it was never a matter of creating a smoothly progressing salvation-history and inviting people to get on board.

Likewise, we radically misunderstand 'apocalyptic' if we suppose that it denotes a way of thinking in the first century in which Israel's history and traditions are done away with and a new world created out of nothing. Apocalyptic, as I have argued in chapter 10 of *The New Testament and the People of God*, is itself radically covenantal: it is precisely because Israel trusts God's covenant promises that she believes he will create new heavens and a new earth, raising his people to life as he does so. It is, of course, perfectly possible to seize on a concept such as 'covenant' and to run it through Paul so that the sharp antitheses between old and new are gently smudged and blurred. But what I mean by Pauline covenantal theology, and what (of course) I think Paul would have meant, includes at its very heart the sense of a secret plan that had to be unveiled in a great, dramatic, and unexpected way. The gospel, says Paul, reveals (the word is *apokaluptetai*) God's covenant faithfulness. Once again, we should beware of false antitheses.

The reason I include these reflections about the pattern and shape of Pauline theology at the start of a chapter about Paul's gospel then and now is that we are always at risk, when we try to grapple with a thinker such as Paul, of assuming too readily that Paul can be fitted into moulds and models which in fact a later age has dreamed up. It is so easy to slip into traditional ways of expounding Paul which in fact distort him. Sometimes, despite the distortions, a lot of the real Paul still remains. But how much better to grasp the actual heart of Paul, and to take the exciting risk of trying to think through ways in which what he actually says may have something to say today and tomorrow. That is what I now propose to attempt. I take three areas, for each of which we have already laid foundations: the gospel, 'justification', and the redefinition of 'God'.

Announcing the King

Proclaiming Jesus Christ as Lord

Paul's gospel must, I believe, be reinstated at the very centre of the church's preaching. The gospel is not, as I have stressed, a set of techniques for making people Christians. Nor is it a set of systematic theological reflections, however important. The gospel is the announcement that Jesus is Lord – Lord of the world, Lord of the cosmos, Lord of the earth, of the ozone layer, of whales and waterfalls, of trees and tortoises. As soon as we get this right we destroy at a stroke the disastrous dichotomy that has existed in people's minds between 'preaching the gospel' on the one hand and what used to be called loosely 'social action' or 'social justice' on the other. Preaching the gospel means announcing Jesus as Lord of the world; and, unless we are prepared to contradict ourselves with every breath we take, we cannot make that announcement without seeking to bring that lordship to bear over every aspect of the world. There was a popular slogan some years ago, according to which 'if Jesus is not Lord of all, he is not Lord at all'. That was routinely applied to personal piety and commitment. I suggest that it is just as true, and just as important, in terms of the cosmic lordship of Jesus.

This means, of course, as it meant for Paul, that there is no area of existence or life, including no area of human life, that does not come up for critique in the light of the sovereignty of the crucified and risen Jesus; no area that is exempt from the summons to allegiance. Perhaps one reason why some have shied away from seeing Jesus' messiahship as a central part of Paul's gospel has been the tacit recognition that it is much easier to turn Christianity into what the Enlightenment wanted it to be – a private system of piety which doesn't impinge on the public world – if the kingship of Jesus is regarded as an unfortunate, and overly Jewish, way of thinking, which Paul and the rest of the early church quickly and thankfully grew out of. I suggest, instead, that the picture Luke paints in Acts is to this extent at least valid. I want to pose the question: what would preachers of the gospel need to do today if people were to say of them what they said of Paul, that he was announcing, in the face of the claims of Caesar, that there was 'another king, namely Jesus'?

They would need, for a start, to do what Paul did, namely, to confront the powers of the world with the news that their time is up, and that they owe allegiance to Jesus himself. This is not so much a matter of telling individual politicians and power-brokers that they need to acknowledge Jesus as the Lord of their own lives, though of course that is important as well. It is more a matter of telling them, in the name of Jesus, that there is a different way of being human, a way characterized by self-giving love, by justice, by honesty, and by the breaking down of the traditional barriers that reinforce the divisions which keep human beings separate from, and as often as not at odds with, one another. And, of course, it is no good saying all this if the church is not saying it by its very life. As I shall suggest presently, this message is at its most powerful when it is presented in symbol and praxis, not merely in dogma and story. This is not a matter, as is sometimes said, of 'bringing politics into religion'. It is bringing the whole world under the lordship of Christ. The gospel message leaves us no choice.

Some more specific examples may just be mentioned. The great prophets of late modernity were, of course, Marx, Freud and Nietzsche. What does the Pauline gospel say about their great themes: money, sex and power?

First, if Jesus is the Lord of all the world, the great god Mammon is not. Preaching the Pauline gospel will mean finding ways of challenging the power of Mammon in our society, and of reminding those who function as his high priests, and those who urge us all to worship at his shrine, that there is another king, namely Jesus. T.S. Eliot asked, fifty-five years ago, whether our modern Western society was founded in fact on anything other than the principle of compound interest; it is a question that looks to me even more urgent today. We live in a society where debt, which used to be regarded as somewhat sordid and shameful, is glitzy and glamorous, with advertisements telling us that when you own a Mastercard 'You've got the whole world in your hands', or alternatively that Visa 'makes the world go round'. Both of them make claims for Mammon which, at the theoretical level, conflict directly with the claims of Jesus, and which, in practice, are very obviously lies; and yet millions believe them, and live by them. At the global level, the problem of debt is notorious and acute, creating misery for millions while it generates millions for a tiny minority. Several church leaders are currently giving their backing and blessing to the project of declaring a year of Jubilee at the Millennium, a year in which major debts would be revoked and everyone could start again. There are of course huge problems with such a scheme, but since the biggest of them is the self-interest of those in positions of power, I fail to see why the churches as a whole could not, as a matter of preaching the gospel of the crucified and risen Jesus, join together in naming the idol Mammon for what he is, and celebrating the love of God in Christ in his place.

Likewise, if Jesus is Lord of the world, the goddess Aphrodite, the goddess of erotic love, is not. Paul confronted this goddess on the streets of every pagan city he visited, just as he would if he came to the Western world of today. Aphrodite's power, which holds millions in its iron grip, promising bliss and giving confusion and misery, must be challenged in Jesus' name.

The problem, of course, is that the church has all too often attempted to talk about sexuality in one of two misleading ways. There is an older dualism which has implied that sexuality is not one of God's great gifts to humankind, and that it must be ignored, denied or repressed. Paul is sometimes accused of holding this view, but that is a grievous slur. Most thinking Christians are today quite well aware of this problem of dualism, and of the damage it causes. Unfortunately, that awareness has led a good many to capitulate to Aphrodite altogether, under the impression that anything else is denial or repression of this God-given instinct. Fear of dualism leads to a semi-or crypto-paganism in which whatever Aphrodite demands, or even suggests, must at once be obeyed, and indeed must be insisted upon as a matter of basic human rights. Such an argument could only hold any force in a world where 'the gospel' has been shrunk to an invitation to personal religious experience, rather than the summons to follow a crucified and risen Messiah. Paul's gospel renounces both dualism and paganism. It summons people to give allegiance to the true king, and to rediscover, through the often painful process of death and rebirth, what genuine self-giving love is all about.

After money and sex, consider power. Once we grasp the nature of Paul's gospel, as I said in a previous chapter, we realize that his material about the 'principalities and powers' is not an extraneous bit of speculation, but close to the very heart of things. We live in a world where still, despite twenty centuries of Christian history, almost everybody assumes that power means, more or less, *force majeur*. Western democracy has for two centuries at least offered what seemed like a stable place between the frightening alternatives of totalitarianism and anarchy. Whether it will continue to do so may depend, I suggest, on the ability of the churches to proclaim that if Jesus is truly the Lord of the world then there is a different sort of power, a more powerful sort of power, a power that is made perfect in weakness.

Of course, at every level of our common life, the suggestion that one might thus actually try to live in what looks like an upside-down mode is regarded as laughable or trivial. This could be simply because it is too frightening. But it could also be because, since Paul's gospel has not been taken seriously, by the churches as much as by anybody else, we have also missed out on Paul's brief redefinition of the place of the magistrate, of the judiciary, within the overarching purposes of God for this between-the-times period of history. Romans 13 is very far from being a charter for big or bullying governments. On the contrary, it places the authorities of this world where they belong: accountable to the one who is Lord of all. In a world where there is still such a thing as great wickedness, we need a judiciary just as we need locks on our front doors. But it must be seen to be accountable to something higher than itself. If it is accountable to the God revealed in Jesus there will be certain quite specific things that follow about the way in which, and the ends for which, it exercises its power.

I regard all this as more or less directly implied by the announcement that Jesus Christ is the Lord of the world. If what Paul says about Jesus is true, those who want to be Pauline Christians in the late twentieth century have no choice but to tackle these issues, and to do so as a matter of urgency.

As a tailpiece in dealing with the contemporary relevance of Paul's gospel, let me repeat something I said earlier. The gospel creates allegiance, not 'experience' *per se*. When we are truly announcing the lordship of Jesus, we must make it clear that, according to this gospel, the one true God has dealt in Jesus Christ with sin, death, guilt and shame, and now summons men and women everywhere to abandon the idols which hold them captive to these things and to discover a new life, and a new way of life, in him. But the gospel is not simply the offer of a new way of being religious. It is not the offer of a certain type of self-fulfilment, or a certain style of religious experience. It is not a take-it-or-leave-it thing, which suggests that people could try this thing on for size and only buy it if the mood takes them. The gospel is the royal announcement. No herald in the ancient world would say 'Tiberius Caesar has become emperor: accept him if it suits you!' The gospel *does* offer a new way of life, which will ultimately be the way of self-fulfilment. But first it offers the cross: the cross of Jesus, and the cross which the risen Lord offers to his followers. The gospel is, then, the announcement about Jesus, not in itself the offer of a new experience. Whatever new experiences result from giving one's allegiance to Jesus are just that, a bunch of new experiences. The only experience guaranteed by Jesus' summons is that of carrying the cross.

'The gospel' leads to 'justification'. How might this central doctrine make fresh sense today?

Justification Then and Now

Justification and community

The gospel creates, not a bunch of individual Christians, but a community. If you take the old route of putting justification, in its traditional meaning, at the centre of your theology, you will always be in danger of sustaining some sort of individualism. This wasn't so much of a problem in Augustine's, or even in Luther's, day, when society was much more bound together than it is now. But both in Enlightenment modernism and in contemporary post-modernism, individualism has been all the rage, with its current symbols of the personal stereo and the privatization of everything. Tragically, some would-be presentations of 'the gospel' have actually bought into this, by implying that one is justified or saved first and foremost as an individual. Paul's gospel could never do that; nor could its corollary, the doctrine of justification. *Of course* every single human being is summoned, in his or her uniqueness, to respond personally to the gospel. Nobody in their right mind would deny that. But there is no such thing as an 'individual' Christian. Paul's gospel created a community; his doctrine of justification sustained it. Ours must do no less.

The ecumenical task

Paul's doctrine of justification by faith impels the churches, in their current fragmented state, into the ecumenical task. It cannot be right that the very doctrine which declares that all who believe in Jesus belong at the same table (Galatians 2) should be used as a way of saying that some, who define the doctrine of justification differently, belong at a different table. The doctrine of justification, in other words, is not merely a doctrine which Catholic and Protestant might just be able to agree on, as a result of hard ecumenical endeavour. It is itself the ecumenical doctrine, the doctrine that rebukes all our petty and often culture-bound church groupings, and which declares that all who believe in Jesus belong together in the one family. Of course there will still be difficulties. Of course we must still have doctrinal debates. But until Christians grasp the message of Galatians 2 (not to mention Romans 14–15, Ephesians 1–3, and sundry other passages), they will still be at first base as far as a true earthing of Paul's theology is concerned. The doctrine of justification is in fact the great *ecumenical* doctrine.

After all, Galatians 2 offers the first great exposition of justification in Paul. In that chapter, the nub of the issue was the question, who are Christians allowed to sit down and eat with? For Paul, that was the question of whether Jewish Christians were allowed to eat with Gentile Christians. Many Christians, both in the Reformation and in the counter-Reformation traditions, have done themselves and the church a great disservice by treating the doctrine of 'justification' as central to their debates, and by supposing that it described the system by which people attained salvation. They have turned the doctrine into its opposite. Justification declares that all who believe in Jesus Christ belong at the same table, no matter what their cultural or racial differences (and, let's face it, a good many denominational distinctions, and indeed distinctions within a single denomination, boil down more to culture than to doctrine). Because what matters is believing in Jesus, detailed agreement on justification itself, properly conceived, isn't the thing which should determine eucharistic fellowship. If Christians could only get this right, they would find that not only would they be believing the gospel, they would be practising it; and that is the best basis for proclaiming it.

Justified without knowing it

There follows from this a vital and liberating point, which I first met in the works of the great Anglican divine Richard Hooker, and for which I shall always be grateful. *One is not justified by faith by believing in justification by faith.* One is justified by faith by believing in Jesus. It follows quite clearly that a great many people are justified by faith who don't know they are justified by faith. The Galatian Christians were in fact justified by faith, though they didn't realize it and thought they had to be circumcised as well. As Hooker said, many pre-Reformation folk were in fact justified by faith, because they believed in Jesus, even though, not knowing about or believing in justification by faith, they lacked assurance, and then sought to fill this vacuum in other ways. Many Christians today may not be very clear about the niceties of doctrine; but, however inarticulately, they hold on to Jesus; and, according to Paul's teaching, they are therefore justified by faith. They are constituted as members of the family. They must be treated as such. This is not to say, of course, that justification is an unimportant or inessential doctrine. Far from it. A church that does not grasp it and teach it is heading for trouble. It is to say that the doctrine of justification itself points away from itself. Believing in Jesus – believing that Jesus is Lord, and the God raised him from the dead – is what counts.

Justification and holiness

If we grasp the gospel and the doctrine of justification in the way I have outlined, there can be no danger, in our theory or practice, of a clash between 'justification by faith' and the Christian obligation to holiness. For centuries now devout Christians, aware of the ever-present danger of Pelagianism, of pride in one's own moral self-worth, have found it difficult to articulate how and why Christians ought to be moral, ought to be holy in thought, word and deed. Sometimes, in their eagerness not to slacken the moral demand, they have in fact slid back into Pelagianism. At other times, perhaps not least at the moment, a half-understood and half-grasped doctrine of justification by faith has been used to shore up an anti-moralism which, even though it occurs within the church, has its roots instead in secular culture, not least within post-modernism.

But this is a travesty. Paul's doctrine of justification is completely dependent upon his gospel, which as we have seen is the proclamation of Jesus as Lord. Allegiance to this Jesus must be total. One of Paul's key phrases is 'the obedience of faith'. Faith and obedience are not antithetical. They belong exactly together. Indeed, very often the word 'faith' itself could properly be translated as 'faithfulness', which makes the point just as well. Nor, of course, does this then compromise the gospel or justification, smuggling in 'works' by a back door. That would only be the case if the re-alignment I have been arguing for throughout were not grasped. Faith, even in this active sense, is never and in no way a qualification, provided from the human side, either for getting into God's family or for staying there once in. It is the God-given badge of membership, neither more nor less. Holiness is the appropriate human condition for those who, by grace alone, find themselves as believing members of the family of God.

Justification and the powers

One of the main polemical thrusts of the doctrine of justification is therefore in a direction quite different from that normally perceived by those who have most stridently defended it. The Pauline doctrine of justification by faith strikes against all attempts to demarcate membership in the people of God by anything other than faith in Jesus Christ; particularly, of course, it rules out any claim to status before God based on race, class or gender. Any attempt to define church membership by anything other than allegiance to Jesus Christ is, quite simply, idolatrous. This was the battle Paul had to fight in Antioch and Galatia, and several other places as well. Here, the thrust of justification is well summed up in Ephesians 3:10, not in terms of what the church must *say* but in terms of what it must *do and be*: through the church, Paul urges, the many-splendoured wisdom of God must be made known to the principalities and powers in the heavenly places. It is by the church living as the one believing community, in which barriers of race, class, gender, and so forth are irrelevant to membership and to holding of office, that the principalities and powers are informed in no uncertain terms that their time is up, that there is indeed a new way of being human. This is, I believe, one of the major contemporary thrusts of justification by faith. And this points us to the larger question: the contemporary relevance of the greatest subject about which Paul wrote.

The Redefinition of God and His Righteousness

What is the relevance for today of Paul's redefinition of the very concept of God itself?

It lies way beyond the scope of this chapter, or even this book, to address the current questions of trinitarian theology, though I note with delight the way in which that subject, which was laughed out of court in some 1960s theology, has been making a strong and lively contribution in the last few years. But I do want to insist that the meaning of the word 'God' should be regarded as one of the central issues in current Christian thinking and preaching.

I said earlier that one of the great changes that has come upon the Western world in the last decade or so is that people have begun to realize, what was always blindingly obvious in Paul's world, that the word 'God' is not univocal. When people say they don't believe in God, it makes sense to ask them which God they don't believe in; when they say they do believe in God, the same question ought to be gently but firmly pressed.

Journalists expressed surprise not long ago when a survey revealed that the great majority of people in the United Kingdom say that they believe in God, but that the same great majority doesn't go to church. They shouldn't have been surprised. The 'God' that the great majority believe in is, pretty certainly, the Deist god, which corresponds in Paul's world to the Epicurean god or gods. These beings were distant, remote, and uncaring. They enjoyed a state of perfect bliss, no doubt; but they never got their hands dirty by caring for, or being active within, the world in which we humans live. It's not surprising that people who believe in the existence of that sort of god don't go to church except now and then. It's hardly worth getting out of bed for a god like that. Paul's announcement of the gospel brought to surprised pagans the news that there was a true God, who was living and active, caring and loving, and who had acted and was acting within history and within human beings to recreate the whole world. Our announcement of the gospel of Jesus must include, as a matter of first importance, the equivalent message: the news that there is a true God who has remained ignored on the margins of our so-called 'Christian' culture, and that this God is made known in and through Jesus of Nazareth, and by the Spirit of Jesus.

This God is so unlike the god of popular Deist imagination that people find it very shocking. What do you mean, they say: God loves us passionately and compassionately? What do you mean, God coming in person to the rescue of the human race? It's indecent; it's illogical; it's untidy. Well, yes, it is – if you start off with eighteenth-century assumptions about what God is like. We need to stop taking the word 'God' for granted in our public discourse and preaching, and show to the world again how the truth to which this word points is known and defined only around Jesus himself.

This will mean, of course, confronting also the false gods that have started bubbling up from the floor in recent years. Theology, like nature, abhors a vacuum. Deism, historically, produces atheism; first you make God a landlord, then he becomes an absentee landlord, then he becomes simply an absentee. But this situation isn't stable; and, pretty soon, you find other, older divinities coming up to take his place. This is, of course, very evident in the New Age movements, some of which are explicitly neo-pagan. Just as Jewish monotheism stood over against dualism, paganism, Epicureanism and Stoicism, so the Christian version of Jewish monotheism must stand, as it did in Paul's preaching, over against all alternative theologies.

Where the New Age has made its greatest inroads has been, I think, at the points where the church has allowed itself to slip into the prevailing dualism, with a distant god and a negative attitude towards creation (including one's own personal bit of creation, that is, one's body). The New Age offers a sudden and exciting reversal of this: creation, including oneself, is divine. Paul's gospel offers the reality of which this is the parody. Creation is not God, but God has made it to reflect his own beauty and, ultimately, to share the freedom of the glory of his children. Human beings are not divine, but they are designed to reflect his own image, and to be filled with his own Spirit.

Addressing these questions is not, of course, a mere matter of getting answers right. Theologies, at this point, determine the way people live, the way they organize the world, the way they treat one another. It could only be within a predominantly Deist culture that the word 'theology' could become, as it has in some quarters of public life, a sneering word for irrelevant theory. If we are claiming, with the Pauline gospel, the high ground of speaking for the one true God, made known in Jesus and the Spirit, then we must be prepared to show how the language of theology relates intimately and vitally to the whole of life, culture, love, art, politics and even religion. This could even mean challenging the academic world in a new way by showing how the study of theology is vitally linked to all other disciplines. (Before that, of course, one would need to persuade the paymasters that such issues were worth spending time on, time that would have to be taken away from the filling in of forms and the conducting of surveys. For that, one would need not only the patience of Job, but the courage to do what I outlined earlier, to confront the principalities and powers with the message that there is a different way of living, and that it is to be taken seriously.)

In particular, the Pauline redefinition of God included, as we saw, the redefinition of the righteousness of God. Though we didn't have space to explore this more fully, the theme in question, as developed in Romans, reaches one particular climax in chapter 8. There, Paul outlines and celebrates the hope that one day the entire cosmos will have its own great exodus, its liberation from bondage to decay. The point is this: the covenant between God and Israel was always designed to be God's means of saving the whole world. It was never supposed to be the means whereby God would have a private little group of people who would be saved while the rest of the world went to hell (whatever you might mean by that). Thus, when God is faithful to the covenant in the death and resurrection of Jesus Christ and in the work of the Spirit, it makes nonsense of the Pauline gospel to imagine that the be-all and end-all of this operation is so that God can have another, merely different, private little group of people who are saved while the world is consigned to the cosmic waste-paper basket. It is not insignificant that the critical passages at this point, the middle of Romans 8 and the middle of 1 Corinthians 15, have themselves often been consigned to a kind of exegetical and theological limbo, with Protestant exegesis in particular appearing quite unsure what to do with them.

I suggest, in fact, that we should be prepared to think through the question of justice – God's justice for the world, in the eventual future, and anticipated in the present – as part of the theme of what we call the righteousness of God. The word *dikaiosune*, after all, can just as easily be translated 'justice' as 'righteousness'. If it is true that God intends to renew the whole cosmos through Christ and by the Spirit – and if that isn't true then Paul is indeed talking nonsense in Romans 8 and 1 Corinthians 15 – then, just as the holiness of Christian living in the present is a proper, albeit partial, fitful and puzzling, anticipation of the future life of the resurrection, so acts of justice, mercy and peace in the present are proper, albeit inevitably partial, fitful and puzzling anticipations of God's eventual design. They are not lost or wasted; they are not, in the old caricature, a matter of oiling the wheels of a machine that is about to run over a cliff. They are signs of hope for a world that groans in travail, waiting for its promised liberation.

When we explore God's righteousness to its very end, it reveals (as we saw) the love of God – the creator's love for the cosmos he has made, and his determination to remake it through the victory of Christ over the powers that deface and distort it. God intends to flood creation with his own love, until the earth is filled with the glory of God as the waters cover the sea. If the gospel reveals the righteousness of God, and if the church is commanded and authorized to announce that gospel, it cannot rest content – for exegetical as well as theological reasons – with anything less than this complete vision. And it cannot therefore rest content while injustice, oppression and violence stalk God's world. After all, Christians are commanded to bring one small piece of creation – their own bodies – into obedience to the healing love of God in Christ. Christians are to live in the present in the light of what God intends us to be in the future. That, as we saw, is what holiness is all about. How can we then not apply the same point to the whole of creation?

Conclusion

Pauline theology, as we can discover it by the time-honoured methods of historical exegesis and theological analysis, is still a vital vehicle for the church's preaching and life. I have not attempted to address the question of what Paul would say to post-modernity; but I think that there, too, Paul would help us to face the challenge with a robust Christian integrity very different from the frightened mutterings one hears in some quarters. Paul's view of truth, of reality, of the self, of the controlling story of the creator and the cosmos, of the covenant God and his covenant people — these can serve very well as the true and vital answer to post-modernity's attempt to deconstruct truth and reality, to destabilize and decentre the self, and to destroy all meta-narratives. I believe, in other words, that Paul's gospel, and the doctrine of justification which follows closely and inescapably from it, have the power to do for the world and the church of today what they did in Paul's own day.

Of course, that will demand persons willing to take the risk of copying Paul: of being wise fools, strong weaklings, failures in human terms. If Christians are to preach the gospel, they cannot expect to be exempt from living the gospel. That, indeed, is part of the message we need to rediscover: that gospel truth is not a matter of ideas only, but of symbol, story and praxis. As Paul himself put it, the kingdom of God is not a matter of talk but of power. So, having attempted to say again what St Paul really said, it is important to remind ourselves that this sort of exercise is only a pointer to the real thing. The gospel of God, today and tomorrow as in Paul's day, is not something to analyze, understand, put in our intellectual pockets and go home content. It is something which, if its very truth is not to be fatally compromised, must become, as it did in Jesus, flesh and blood. That which was unveiled before an unprepared world in Jesus Christ must be unveiled again and again, as those who believe in Jesus Christ live by the Spirit and, in life as well as in word, announce the gospel to the world.

CHAPTER 10

Paul, Jesus and Christian Origins

We are now in a position to address the question which hangs over the whole detailed study of Paul. Was Paul really 'the founder of Christianity'? Did he, in other words, invent Christianity as we now know it, transforming the beliefs and vocation of Jesus of Nazareth into a system and movement which Jesus himself would never have recognized? Is it to him that we owe two thousand years of Christian history, with all its puzzles and paradoxes, its glories and its shame?

Among many writers, at both scholarly and popular levels, who have argued this case, there is one recent book which pushes the point into the public eye, and I shall take it as my main conversation partner in this concluding chapter. A.N. Wilson, a prolific writer of novels and biographies, has recently produced a book entitled *Paul: The Mind of the Apostle*.[1] It is a learned, witty and interesting treatment, full of the local colour of Paul's travels and the places he visited, full (as well) of fascinating speculations about what made Paul tick. Wilson is clearly fascinated by Paul, as well one might be; but he declares his writings to be ultimately 'incomprehensible', suggesting that the letters 'are written from a point of view of one whose life is wracked by self-contradiction, whose life is pulled in two conflicting directions' (56f.). Paul had a 'restless and almost Nietzschean mind' (122f.); in his 'brilliantly tormented view of the human condition' (122) he had thought himself into an 'extreme position of metaphysical isolation' (124).

For Paul, he suggests, 'Christ' had little or nothing to do with the historical Jesus. 'The historicity of Jesus became unimportant from the moment Paul had his apocalypse' (73). The word 'Christ' became a cipher for an ideal, a religious interiority, 'the highest aspiration of which the human heart is or feels capable' (221). Christ, for Paul, 'was not so much

167

the man [the Jerusalem Christians] remembered (though of course he was that) but a presence of divine love in the hearts of believers' (207). This, for Wilson, is not actually an unmitigated disaster: Paul's theology may have had little to do with the man from Nazareth, but at least he transformed what would otherwise have remained a time-bound, local and political message into a religion of the heart that was available to people anywhere and at any time (233). 'The sayings of Jesus can shock us but they scarcely represent a cohesive oral framework on which we can base our lives. The religion of Paul, by contrast, wild, ecstatic and confused as it must often appear… contains all the makings of a religion with universal appeal' (239). This, it seems, was the beginning of what we know as Christianity. For the Gentile followers of Paul, 'the word Christ was synonymous not with the Anointed Jewish Deliverer of Israel, so much as with an inner known God, a hidden Saviour, a Blessed Sacrament called Jesus' (132). In all this, Wilson manages nevertheless to salvage some continuity with Jesus, but at a high level of abstraction. 'While the Petrines, the Palestinians, clung to the memory of Jesus, Paul was able to apply, as a universalized creed, the perceptions of heaven which were perhaps Jesus' own: the confidence that each individual could turn to God as to a Father and meet a response of love' (239).

Where, then, did Paul get this new religion from? Wilson never glimpses Saul the Shammaite Pharisee, as we have expounded his pre-Christian life in chapter 2 above. Instead he invents an interesting new character. He envisages a Saul who grew up in the midst of pagan religion in Tarsus, knowing particularly the Mithraic rituals and the worship of the divine Herakles. He then, going to Jerusalem, entered the employ of the chief priests, and acted as a temple servant. In that capacity, he undoubtedly saw and heard Jesus himself, and undoubtedly knew about, perhaps even witnessed, his crucifixion. He may even have helped to arrest Jesus. He was a collaborator with Rome.

As he reflected on what he had, perhaps, helped to bring about, Paul's mind and imagination was caught up into categories taken from pagan worship. The devotees of Mithras, bathed with the blood of a sacrificial bull, found that 'as the blood flowed down from their victim, they derived strength from it, divine strength; and they were thereby initiated into secrets, buried long since in the depths of the earth and now made manifest'. Thus when, in the years that followed, 'the Crucifixion became the focus of Paul's obsessive religious attention', 'he would mythologize it, and try to come to terms with its meaning' (60). Paul brought together the thought of Mithras and the thought of the crucified Jesus, and found himself identified with the latter: 'In the mind of the Romanized Jew, the tormented Pharisee, the temple guard and tentmaker for the legions, it was Paul himself who was nailed to that instrument of torture, Paul who died, Paul who suffered, Paul who rose' (60; cf. 71, 77f., 122). The Mithras-cult was the basis of Paul's invention of the Christian eucharist, which Wilson manages both to disparage as a mere innovation, unrelated to the Jesus of history, and to admire as a remarkably influential cultural phenomenon (165-68). Similarly, Paul borrowed the idea of the demi-god Herakles as the model for his picture of the dying and rising Jesus (71, 258).

Paul's own religious experience was 'comparable to that mania which took possession of the initiates into a mystery' (76). The image of 'seeing through a glass darkly', coming at the end of Paul's most famous poem (1 Corinthians 13), would have made pagan converts feel right at home (173f.). Paul, in other words, turned the fact of Jesus' crucifixion into the basis of a new mystery religion. He mythologized Jesus: he 'was able to draw out the mythological implications of an old religion… and to construct therefrom a myth with reverberations much wider than the confines of Palestinian Judaism' (72).

Once Paul became a preacher and a missionary, his horizon, according to Wilson, was dominated by this mythological construct and by the pressing need to make other people share it. At the same time, there was another pressing need: to get the job done before the end of the world, which all early Christians believed was imminent (93, 108, 141, etc.). This coming end was 'the most fundamental of all Paul's beliefs' (177). Wilson envisages a Paul who is constantly aware that the end, the parousia, the second coming of Jesus, might happen at any moment, and who indeed goes to Jerusalem to try to force God's hand. The messianic prophecies are to be fulfilled through his, Paul's, own work (206). For Paul, 'resurrection' is not primarily something that happened to Jesus in the recent past, but something that is soon to happen to him and to everyone else, a burning hope that colours everything he does. But when Paul actually arrives in Jerusalem, and is arrested following a riot, he begins to suspect that the apocalypse has gone wrong (212): the coming hadn't happened as it should have done (207, 218). (There is a certain tension here, since Wilson also thinks (193) that, when writing Romans, i.e. before his last journey to Jerusalem, Paul imagined that maybe the end would come as a result of his trip to Spain.) Paul therefore goes to Rome with a message now more confused, and more agonized, than before. But, though we do not know what actually became of him there, his legacy was assured. He, not Jesus, was — if anyone was — 'the Founder of Christianity' (258).

Problems with the Portrait

Wilson's picture of Paul is engaging, not altogether unsympathetic, extremely colourful, and intriguing. It leaves the reader wanting to ask more questions, to reread Paul, to think about what he said and why. He hears in Paul a note which should not be muted — a note of love, of personal faith, of a devotion which springs from the heart and calls (despite the surface noise of all sorts of other things) to other hearts. For all this we must be grateful. His historical reconstructions bring the apostle to life in three dimensions — even if he seems to be confused about the detail from time to time, as when he imagines that the Jerusalem water supply came from Jericho (43). He is aware of some bits of recent Pauline scholarship — though he attempts to have his cake and eat it on various issues, by (for instance) trying to combine the position of E.P. Sanders, according to whom Judaism was not a religion of legalistic works-righteousness, with the position Sanders has devastatingly undermined, that Paul's polemic against Judaism was really an opposition to 'religion' as such (e.g. 195, 209).

But these are comparatively minor comments. We must come to some central details. There are several crucial points where Wilson's portrait of Paul needs serious questioning.

Saul's background

To begin with, it is historically out of the question that Saul of Tarsus should have been a collaborator with Rome, a servant of the high priest. Wilson bases this conjecture on Acts 9:1-2, 14, 21, 26:10-12, which say that Saul obtained authority from the chief priests for his persecuting mission in Damascus. But this is completely to misunderstand the political situation and the different players in it. The Shammaite Pharisees, as we saw, were the hard-liners, bitterly opposed to collaboration, and indeed fiercely supportive of revolutionary movements. This is what was meant by 'zeal', which the pre-Christian Saul of Tarsus possessed in abundance.

But a Pharisee, of whatever party, had no official authority to act in such a way. The Pharisees were a pressure group, not the ruling body within Judaism. Even if a Pharisee was a member of the Sanhedrin, any authority he possessed would be in virtue of that membership, not of being a Pharisee. So when the zealous Saul of Tarsus, frustrated and religiously offended at the rapid spread of the new superstition that was leading people away from the study of Torah and the defence of the Temple, boiled over with desire to act violently against such wickedness, he had no means of doing so within the law – unless he went to the hated quislings, the high priests, and obtained official documentation sanctioning his marauding venture. The high priests cared about new movements within Jerusalem. Such things posed an immediate threat to law and order, a subversive element which might bring Roman troops out onto the streets. But we have no reason to suppose that they cared two figs about what went on in Damascus. Not so the zealous ultra-right Pharisee Saul. The author of Galatians 1 and Philippians 3 would have laughed a long, hollow laugh at the thought of being a collaborator, in the pay of the high priests.

Judaism and Hellenism

Underneath Wilson's whole reconstruction, despite his occasional protestation (e.g. 72), we discover, in fact, the most serious weaknesses of the old history-of-religions school. He assumes, throughout, that Judaism was a local, almost tribal religion, while the various forms of Hellenism were universal systems or philosophies. Paul translated Jesus' message from Judaism to Hellenism, so that all could join in. Hence the old jibe (which Wilson repeats) that nobody really understood Paul except the second-century heretic Marcion, and even he misunderstood him. (Marcion, we may recall, reinvented Christianity as a non- and even anti-Jewish religion.) This is a dangerous half-truth, and the wrong half at that. Wilson constantly suggests that Paul left behind Judaism, Jewish Christians, and Jerusalem. He even allows himself to say that Paul 'turned his back on Palestinian Judaism' (136), at the very point when, in the story that Wilson is following, Paul was beginning the arduous and complex task of taking a collection, from the Gentile churches, precisely for the Jewish Christians who lived in Palestine.

As we saw earlier in this book, Paul grasped something which was and is fundamental to Judaism, but which historians of 'religion' – ironically, in the

Hellenistic tradition – have always found very difficult to get their minds round: that if the one God of Judaism was also the creator of the whole world, and if his call of Israel to be his people was his chosen way of addressing the problems of the whole world, then *the world did not need a non-Jewish message*. The world had enough of them already. The world needed the *Jewish* message – that the one true God had conquered the idols the world had worshipped, and had thereby thrown open the prison doors behind which the whole human race had languished.

This means that, at a stroke, Wilson's fanciful theories about Mithras and Herakles are rendered as unnecessary as they were in any case unlikely. Paul, of course, knew plenty about pagan religion; he speaks in 1 Corinthians 8 of 'gods many and lords many', and in Acts 17 Luke credibly portrays him being stirred in his spirit, as a good ex-Shammaite might well be, at the sight of all the idolatry of Athens. As we saw in the first chapter, attempts have been made at various stages to derive parts of Paul's religion and theology from the world of pagan philosophy and mystery-religions. All have failed, as virtually all Pauline scholars now recognize. It is not so much that Wilson is trying to lock the door after the horse has bolted. He is trying to ride across open country on a hobby-horse.

Cross and resurrection

These strange and improbable guesses as to the sources of Paul's ideas about the significance of Jesus have, of course, come in to fill the vacuum created by Wilson's failure to understand the actual meaning, for Paul, of the death and resurrection of Jesus. As we saw in chapter 3, this was not a matter of strange mystical speculation. It was a matter of eschatological fulfilment. The purpose of the one true God for Israel had come true, precisely in these events. This is the single largest issue which is missing from Wilson's reconstruction, and it skews the whole project much as would be done if one tried to draw a map of Europe forgetting about France. Everything else is the wrong shape, the borders don't work, and trying to reconstruct European history becomes a matter of wild guesses and elaborate and unlikely reconstructions.

For Paul, the resurrection of Jesus was the great eschatological event. Wilson manages to write a whole book on Paul without even noticing this; indeed, asserting at one point that Paul has no place for the bodily resurrection of Jesus (236). For him, 'resurrection' in Paul is an idea, a belief, a future hope, rather than something that has actually happened. His Paul could never have written, 'If Christ is not raised, our preaching is empty and so is your faith... if Christ is not raised, your faith is futile and you are still in your sins' (1 Corinthians 15:14, 17). His Paul would never have outlined a careful scheme of eschatological events, beginning with the resurrection and lordship of Jesus the Messiah as something that had already happened, was already the case (1 Corinthians 15:20-28). Paul was not living merely in the last days, the frantic time before the messianic prophecies were to be fulfilled. He was living in the first days, the time immediately after those prophecies had all come true. 'All the promises of God are "yes" in him', he wrote (2 Corinthians 1:20); it didn't look like he, as a Pharisee, had expected it would, but the resurrection left him no choice but to conclude that in fact 'the righteousness of God', the great overarching covenant plan from Abraham to the final redemption, had already been unveiled in the events, the messianic events, of Jesus' life, death and resurrection.

Paul did not turn the resurrection of Jesus from being a physical event into being a Hellenistic-style mystery. He understood it Jewishly through and through. He discovered that, precisely because Israel was the focal point of the creator's dealings with his world, what the creator had done in and through Jesus he had done for the whole world. Instead of Wilson's dubious derivations, we find once more (as I outlined in chapter 5) the notion of polemical engagement. Paul 'takes every thought captive to obey Christ' (2 Corinthians 10:5). Start with Hellenism, and the picture falls apart. Start with Judaism, and stay within it, and the picture, Hellenistic analogies included, falls into place.

The same is true of what Paul came to realize about the crucifixion of Jesus. Setting up partial and misleading parallels between what Paul says about the facts and meaning of Jesus' death and the rituals of the mystery religions is an attempt to turn the clock back in a way now forbidden by the most massive and learned studies of the subject (e.g. A.J.M. Wedderburn, *Baptism and Resurrection*).[2] But that is nothing to what Wilson misses. In a revealing page (57), discussing Galatians 3:13-14, he describes Paul's assertion that 'Christ became a curse for us' as 'one of his more incomprehensible flights of imagery', and suggests that crucifixion was a curse not because of the Jewish law but because of the Roman law. This, be it noted, despite the fact that Paul quotes the passage in the Jewish law (Deuteronomy 21:23) in which the curse is explicitly announced – and

Wilson quotes him quoting it! Nevertheless, he concludes that 'the "scandal" of the cross... is a Roman scandal' (58).

This betrays a deep-seated misapprehension both of the Jewish context and of Paul's reworking of it. There are Jewish texts which speak with horror of previous crucifixions, precisely because of the Deuteronomic curse. But for Paul the issue in Galatians 3, which despite Wilson's assertion is certainly not inexplicable to commentators (how many commentaries on Galatians, one wonders, has Wilson actually read?), is: what happens to the promises to Abraham, the promises that God would give him a worldwide family, when Abraham's family are faced with the curse of the law? This is a thoroughly Jewish question, and Paul gives it a thoroughly Jewish answer – but an answer, we note again, which is both *about* God's reaching out to the whole world and itself *addressed to* the whole world, specifically here to ex-pagans in Galatia.

The answer hinges, as I have shown in detail elsewhere,[3] on Paul's foundational belief that Jesus, so far from being irrelevant for theology, was in fact the Jewish Messiah, the one in whose life, death and resurrection Israel's destiny was summed up and brought to fulfilment. He has carried the destiny of Israel, including the promises to Abraham, down into the valley of death, down into the place of the curse, on behalf of Israel and hence of the whole world. The nearest analogies to this in non-Christian writings are not in Roman or Greek culture but in the Jewish literature about the martyrs. One might consult, to begin with, 2 Maccabees 7:36-38, or 4 Maccabees 6:27-29, 17:20-22.

Paul, as we saw, has a thoroughly worked out theology of the cross, integrated completely with the other elements of his 'gospel'. (Any lexicon would have told Wilson, by the way, that Paul did not 'coin' the word 'gospel', as he suggests (150), any more than he invented the word *agape* for 'love' (84).) The cross was the moment when the one true God defeated the principalities and powers, in accordance with Jewish prophecy; it was therefore the moment when sin and death themselves were defeated. 'The Messiah died for our sins according to the scriptures.' In particular, it was the moment when the sin that had stood in the account against both Jew and Gentile was dealt with as it deserved, in the person of the one faithful Israelite, the Messiah in whom Israel's vocation and destiny (to be the means of saving the world) was summed up and realized (Romans 3:21-26). It was the moment when the condemnation of God was executed upon sin itself (Romans 8:3). It is frankly impossible to see how any of these trains of thought could have been generated, let alone sustained, by the process which Wilson imagines. It is easier by far, historically, exegetically and theologically, to suppose that Paul the Jew reflected Jewishly, in the light of the Jewish scriptures on the one hand and the resurrection of Jesus on the other, on the claim that Jesus was indeed the Jewish Messiah, in whom the promises had been fulfilled. Easier by far to recognize that he came quickly to see that the claim was not only true, but relevant as it stood to the whole world, not least the pagan world where the essentially Jewish message of the deep and passionate love of the creator God for his whole creation was neither known nor imagined.

Perhaps the most telling and self-contradictory feature of the whole picture is that, though Wilson tries to make Paul more and more a Hellenist, he attempts also to retain in Paul that which, however we interpret it, was undoubtedly a Jewish rather than a Greek idea, that of eschatology. I have argued elsewhere that this eschatology did not mean 'the end of the world' in the normally accepted sense; but, however we interpret it, it makes no sense within the world of a new sort of Hellenistic mystery-religion. On this whole question the best comment remains, still, that of Albert Schweitzer, writing in a book which Wilson would have done well to ponder deeply:

> Since all [Paul's] conceptions and thoughts are rooted in eschatology, those who labour to explain him on the basis of Hellenism, are like a man who should bring water from a long distance in leaky watering-cans in order to water a garden lying beside a stream.[4]

For Paul, the cross and resurrection were *the* eschatological events *par excellence*. He knew that God would, one day, complete the work he had begun both in the cosmos (Romans 8; 1 Corinthians 15), and in him personally, as in all believers (Philippians 1:6). He knew, too, that events were looming on the historical scene which would be, along with the resurrection of Jesus, part of the eschatological inbreaking of the Age to Come (2 Thessalonians 2). But he knew, above all and more than all, that the Age to Come had already dawned when Jesus of Nazareth defeated death. That was what mattered. The outworkings and implications demanded energy and application, and even suffering and facing persecution. But all was done with a note of joy: nothing could now separate those in Christ from the all-powerful, all-embracing, all-conquering love of the creator and covenant God.

Jesus and God

Which leads us, of course, to Christology. At the heart of Paul's picture of Jesus, as we saw in chapter 4, stands his redefinition of monotheism, with Jesus within it. Wilson (like, we should note, a good many scholars) is committed to seeing any attempt to place Jesus and God side by side as a step away from Jewish monotheism and towards a kind of paganism. He wrestles interestingly with Philippians 2:5-11 (113-15), noting just how early this obviously 'high' Christology actually is – i.e. long before the Fourth Gospel, and quite possibly before Paul himself. But he fails to see what precisely Paul has done here, placing Jesus *within* a firmly scriptural statement of Jewish monotheism itself. Instead, he suggests that those who read such a passage would think naturally of a figure like Dionysus, 'who walked the earth concealing his own divinity', and supposes that this figure 'replaces the actual or folk-memory of the Galilean preacher' (114).

Wilson does not appear quite satisfied with that explanation, partly because of the poem being so early. But he has no alternative to propose. He constantly hints and suggests that any ascription of divinity to Jesus belongs on a trajectory away from Judaism and into the world of paganism; but, as we saw in chapter 4, the truth is very different. It was precisely when Paul was standing firm against paganism – against pagan cult in 1 Corinthians 8, against pagan empire in Philippians 2, and against pagan principalities and powers in Colossians 1 – that he places Jesus within statements of Jewish monotheism. This cannot be accidental. Paul cannot have failed to have known what he was doing at this point. All right, it was risky. He must have known that some of his hearers would misunderstand, would think (as they did in Athens) that he was peddling news of one or two foreign deities ('Jesus and Anastasis' (Acts 17:18): *anastasis* was, of course, the Greek for 'resurrection', and the passage holds out the intriguing possibility that some Athenians thought Paul was talking about two divine beings, one male and one female). Paul would have claimed that he had to take the risk. The fact of Jesus' resurrection, understood in the light not of nebulous mystical experience but of the Jewish scriptures themselves, left him with no choice. Jesus the Jewish Messiah was the reality of which all pagan idols were the parody. Jesus the Jewish Messiah, in whom the God of Israel had become known personally, face to face – this Jesus was the reality towards which all Israel's history, tradition, prophecy, suffering and expectation had been pointing.

A distorting image

For all Wilson's learning and subtlety of reconstruction, then, his portrait of Paul fails at several crucial points. Historically, he offers a hypothesis about Paul's background, conversion and the development of his religious thought that is unconvincing in itself and ignores the alternative explanations which lie ready to hand. Theologically, he proposes a reconstruction of Paul's thought which leaves out its major features (the fulfilment of the promises in the events of Jesus, especially his death and resurrection, and the revelation of the God of Israel, and his 'righteousness', in Jesus himself) and fills the gap with theories about tortured imaginings and speculative fantasy. Exegetically, he offers some interesting reflections on various letters, notably Philippians, for which he obviously has a real and understandable affection (217-21). But when it comes to the real test case, namely Romans, Wilson does not even begin to penetrate its mysteries, despite having an obvious admiration for the letter (192-98). This is hardly surprising, since in his historical and theological constructs he has explicitly ruled out looking for the key in the place where it is to be found: in Paul's wrestling with the covenant promises of the God of Israel, which he believed had been fulfilled in the death and resurrection of the Jewish Messiah.

History, theology, exegesis; what of application? It is never completely clear whether Wilson likes Paul or dislikes him, whether he is commending him to us or warning us against him. Does he approve of Paul (with major reservations), or disapprove of him (with major concessions)? Is he blaming Paul for muddling up the message of Jesus, or is he commending him for making it available to a wider audience? Is he accusing Paul of turning Christianity into a 'religion', or is he commending him for opposing 'religion' both of the Jewish sort and of the later Christian sort? Is he damning Paul with faint praise, or praising him with faint damns? Is it, after all, really Paul who is muddled and contradictory? Wilson seems to value Christianity as a wonderful, world-shaping cultural artefact, while rejecting it as an actual practical proposition in anything like its contemporary form. He reserves especial scorn for the Anglicanism he so firmly renounced some years ago, which would, he says, have been for Paul 'the ultimate absurdity – more ridiculous than any of the other forms of "Christianity" which would have filled him with despair' (195f.).

At the same time, there remains a yearning question mark. Wilson sees so much of Paul in terms of muddle, self-contradiction, empty rhetoric and bombast – 'The spiritual Mr Toad gets out his big drum and beats and bangs it for all he is worth' (217) – totally ignoring the purpose of Philippians 3:4-6 in the developing argument. Yet he still retains a sense that within Paul, despite all, there may be something which is of great value, of ultimate worth. He seems to hear, again and again, a note, a clear call, which none of the extraneous noise has been able to drown out. It is the note of love: the love of God, offered freely to all in Jesus Christ, reaching out to the ends of the earth, ready to be accepted by any human being of whatever background, ready to transform human life into something deeper and richer. At this point, as we saw, he is prepared to allow that Jesus and Paul speak with one voice (239).

Wilson is right to hear this note. He is right to see (221) that at this point Paul is more than a philosopher – though wrong, perhaps, to limit that 'more' to the suggestion that Paul is 'the first romantic poet in history'. Still, if romantic poetry is for Wilson a window on the love of the creator God, let us affirm that too. Just as, in his book on Jesus, Wilson recognized some crucial elements of the truth, albeit set within a series of misunderstandings, so here he has glimpsed some flashes of light, which, if he were to follow them carefully, would lead him out of the fog of speculation and into a fuller, more rounded, and far more satisfying picture of Paul than the one he has described. And then, who knows what else might happen?

All of which leads us to the greatest question of all, to which Wilson's book does not, after all, make the contribution that he intended. What is the relation between Paul, Jesus and the origins of Christianity?

From Jesus to Paul – and Beyond

It all depends, of course, not just on what you make of Paul but on what you make of Jesus. I have written at length on this topic elsewhere, most recently in *Jesus and the Victory of God*.[5] In the light of that, it should be clear where the discussion has to start.

If we are to locate both Jesus and Paul within the world of first-century Judaism, within the turbulent theological and political movements and expectations of the time (and if we are not then we should admit that we know very little about either of them) then we must face the fact that neither of them was teaching a timeless system of religion or ethics, or even a timeless message about how human beings are saved. Both of them believed themselves to be actors within the drama staged by Israel's God in fulfilment of his long purposes. Both, in other words, breathed the air of Jewish eschatology.

It will not do, therefore, to line up 'Jesus' key concepts' and 'Paul's key concepts' and play them off against one another. It will not do to point out that Jesus talked about repentance and the coming kingdom, while Paul talked about justification by faith. It misses the point even to show (though this can be done quite easily) that these two, when set in context and translated into terms of one another, belong extremely closely together. The point is that Jesus believed himself to be called to a particular role in the eschatological drama; and so did Paul. The real question is, what were those roles, and how might they relate?

I have argued elsewhere that Jesus believed himself called to be the one through whom God's strange purposes for Israel would reach their ordained climax. He announced to Israel that the long-awaited kingdom had arrived. He celebrated it with all who would join him, welcoming them into table-fellowship and assuring them that their sins were forgiven. But the kingdom would not look like Jesus' contemporaries had imagined. It would not endorse their particular agendas. Particularly, it would not underwrite the agendas of those who were bent on 'zeal', on forcing upon Israel a hard and exclusive piety, an all-or-nothing stand for God, Torah, Land and Temple that would commit Israel to a war of liberation against Rome. Jesus warned that to take this route would result in huge, unmitigated disaster; and that this disaster, if Israel brought it down upon her own head, would have to be seen as the wrath of Israel's God against his people. Such actions would mean that the perpetrators had translated their vocation to be the light of the world into a vocation to be the judges of the world. Those who judged would themselves be judged. Those who took the sword would perish with the sword. Those who turned the Temple into a den of brigands would only have themselves to blame when the Temple itself was torn down, so that not one stone was left upon another.

But Jesus did not remain as a spectator, commenting on this passage of events from outside. He came to the centre of the stage, not just metaphorically, but literally, in his entry to Jerusalem and his Temple-action. His dramatic action symbolized his belief that he was called to be the Messiah, the one through whom Israel's destiny would be realized. (We need, perhaps, to remind ourselves that within a hundred years or so of

179

Jesus there were at least a dozen others who believed themselves to be the Messiah.) He had authority over the Temple. The house of God might be destroyed, but he would be vindicated. Yet, as he clearly knew, by his symbolic action he was calling down upon himself the fate he had predicted for the Temple. He would suffer as so many Jewish martyrs had suffered, handed over to the pagans for slaughter. Yet, conscious of his vocation, he enacted another great symbol: the new exodus, the great liberation, encoded in a final Passover meal with his followers. He would draw on to himself the coming cataclysm, thus making a way through, whereby the encroaching evil would be defeated, Israel would be liberated, and the saving purpose of Israel's God for the whole world might at last be realized.

As he trod this road, Jesus was conscious of a deeper vocation even than that of Messiah. Israel's greatest hope was that YHWH, her God, would return to her in person, coming to Zion as judge and redeemer. In Jesus' last great journey to Jerusalem, in his action in the Temple and the Upper Room, he dramatically symbolized that return. It looks as though he intended to enact and embody that which, in Israel's scriptures, YHWH had said he would do in person. There could be no greater claim; yet the claim, though stupendous, only made sense within, could only be made from within, the context of the first-century Jewish world that bounded all Jesus' thoughts and actions. He went to his death believing that the hopes and fears of Israel and the world would thereby be drawn together once and for all. This would be the great event, the culmination of Israel's history, the redemption, the new exodus. This was how the kingdom would come.

Like any Jewish martyr of the period, Jesus believed firmly that if he died in obedience to the will of God he would be vindicated by being raised from the dead. Unlike other martyrs, he seems to have believed that, since what he was doing was special, climactic, the one-off moment of Israel's salvation, his resurrection would come without delay. He would be raised 'on the third day'. Like the other things Jesus believed, this makes perfect, though startling, sense within the worldview of a first-century Jew aware of a vocation to be the means through which God would do for his people at last that which he had always promised.

It should be clear from all this that if Paul had simply trotted out, parrot-fashion, every line of Jesus' teaching – if he had repeated the parables, if he had tried to do again what Jesus did in announcing and inaugurating the kingdom – he would not have been endorsing Jesus, as an appropriate and loyal follower should. He would have been denying him. Someone who copies exactly what a would-be Messiah does is himself trying to be a Messiah; which means denying the earlier claim. When we see the entire sequence within the context of Jewish eschatology, we are forced to realize that for Paul to be a loyal 'servant of Jesus Christ', as he describes himself, could never mean that Paul would repeat Jesus' unique, one-off announcement of the kingdom to his fellow Jews. What we are looking for is not a parallelism between two abstract messages. It is the *appropriate continuity* between two people living, and conscious of living, at different points in the eschatological timetable.

Jesus believed it was his vocation to bring Israel's history to its climax. Paul believed that Jesus had succeeded in that aim. Paul believed, in consequence of that belief and as part of his own special vocation, that he was himself now called to announce to the whole world that Israel's history had been brought to its climax in that way. *When Paul announced 'the gospel' to the Gentile world, therefore, he was deliberately and consciously implementing the achievement of Jesus.* He was, as he himself said, building on the foundation, not laying another one (1 Corinthians 3:11). He was not 'founding a separate religion'. He was not inventing a new ethical system. He was not perpetrating a timeless scheme of salvation, a new mystery-religion divorced from the real, human Jesus of Nazareth. He was calling the world to allegiance to its rightful Lord, the Jewish Messiah now exalted as the Jewish Messiah was always supposed to be. A new mystery religion, focused on a mythical 'lord', would not have threatened anyone in the Greek or Roman world. 'Another king', the human Jesus whose claims cut directly across those of Caesar, did.

This reminds us that neither for Jesus nor for Paul was the message, the announcement, a matter merely of 'religion'. The post-enlightenment box into which 'religion' has been slotted, whether by those determined to make religion irrelevant to real life or by those determined to protect religion from the ravages of real life, has nothing to do with the worldview of a first-century Jew believing that Israel's God, the creator, was taking his power and reigning. Jesus was not announcing 'a new religion'; nor was Paul. Nor was the Judaism whose expectation both were affirming a matter of 'religion' only. Of course (lest ears be so dull that they translate what I am saying into its opposite) — *of course* the proclamation of Jesus, and the gospel announcement of Paul, addressed human beings with a challenge and a summons, a warning and an offer, which went down to the very depths of human experience, into the far recesses of the heart, awakening parts which other messages could not reach. But they did this, not because they were about 'religion' as divorced from the rest of life, but because the claim of Israel always was, the message of Jesus always was, and the announcement of Paul always was, that the human race was to be shown, invited to, summoned into, and enabled to discover the true way of being human, the way to reflect the very image of God himself in every aspect of life and with every fibre of one's being. If that is what you mean by 'religion', so be it. Jesus and Paul thought of it as Life, as being human, as being the children of God.

When all this is said and done, it should be comparatively easy to work through the actions and message of Jesus, and the agenda and letters of Paul, and to show that there is between them, not (of course) a one-for-one correspondence, but a coherence, an appropriate correlation, an integration that allows fully for the radically different perspective of each. Jesus was bringing Israel's history to its climax; Paul was living in the light of that climax. Jesus was narrowly focused on the sharp-edged, single task; Paul was celebrating the success of that task, and discovering its fruits in a thousand different ways and settings. Jesus believed he had to go the incredibly risky route of acting and speaking in such a way as to imply that he was embodying the judging and saving action of YHWH himself; Paul wrote of Jesus in such a way as to claim that Jesus was indeed the embodiment of the one God of Jewish monotheism.

No doubt there are dozens of different details to be examined carefully if the question of Jesus and Paul is to be sewn up in all its particulars. To go further into the question at this point is unnecessary; it has been done so well, so recently, by David Wenham in his book *Paul: Follower of Jesus or Founder of Christianity*[6] that it would be tedious to traverse the same ground again. Despite the popular impression, there are in fact a good many echoes of the actual sayings of Jesus in the letters of Paul, though here again Paul has not been a slavish repeater of tradition so much as faithful rethinker of the rich material he has heard, using it in fresh ways for his own very different context. What matters, far above any attempts to place Jesus and Paul one on each side of a theological see-saw and make them balance out, is to grasp the truth that grasped them both: that in their day, and through their agency – the one as focus, the other as pointer – the one living and true God had acted climactically and decisively to liberate Israel and the world, and to establish his kingdom of love, the kingdom through which the world would be brought out of the long winter of sin and death and would taste at last the fruits of the Age to Come.

Paul, of course, believed that he was living in the very early days of spring. Almost all the ice and snow still remained to be melted. Looking at the world nearly two thousand years later, one may suggest that we have got no further (in Northern hemisphere terms!) than March at the latest. Some places have felt real sunshine, have seen flowers and blossoms which show that winter is really over. Other places remain icebound. Some places experienced early blooms, but the snow has covered them again. Part of the point of the new age, it seems, is that it doesn't conform to a timetable like the natural seasons. The creation, after all, is to be set free from its timetables of life and death, its bondage to decay. But, as Paul insists in the same passage where he asserts that great hope, this will happen through the witness, the holiness, the suffering, the prayer, and finally the resurrection of those in whose hearts God has already brought about 'the first-fruits of the Spirit' (Romans 8:18-27). So, as he says in another great passage of hope, 'be steadfast, immovable, always abounding in the work of the Lord; since you know that, in the Lord, your labour is not in vain' (1 Corinthians 15:58). That, as Paul well knew, is the appropriate attitude and activity for those who, whether suffering or celebrating, live in the period between the triumph of Calvary and Easter and the day when God will be all in all.

Notes

1. A.N. Wilson, *Paul: The Mind of the Apostle,* 1997. Page references in what follows are to this work.
2. A.J.M. Wedderburn, *Baptism and Resurrection: Studies in Pauline Theology against its Graeco-Roman Background*, 1987.
3. N.T. Wright, *The Climax of the Covenant*, 1991, chapter 7.
4. Albert Schweitzer, *The Mysticism of Paul the Apostle*, 1968, page 140.
5. N.T. Wright, *Jesus and the Victory of God,* 1996.
6. David Wenham, *Paul: Follower of Jesus or Founder of Christianity,* 1995.

Annotated Bibliography

This bibliography is of books about Paul and his letters and theology, rather than commentaries on the letters themselves. The list for those would be at least as long again! One work which is of great value on almost all biblical topics, Pauline included, is the new 6-volume *Anchor Bible Dictionary*, edited by D.N. Freedman (Doubleday, 1992). There are of course literally hundreds of articles on Pauline subjects in the journals, and some of them are very important. But one has to start somewhere.

For those who are literally starting from scratch, and want a user-friendly introduction to the subject, some suitable books are marked with an asterisk (*).

Beker, J. Christiaan, *Paul the Apostle: The Triumph of God in Life and Thought,* Fortress, 1980.

> A somewhat rambling and disjointed, but nevertheless powerful, presentation of an American version of Käsemann's theological treatment of Paul.

*Beker, J. Christiaan, *Paul's Apocalyptic Gospel: The Coming Triumph of God,* Fortress, 1982.

> A shorter and more popular presentation of the following title. Beker argues that Paul's theology is dominated by the coming apocalyptic event of God's triumph over the world.

Boyarin, Daniel, *A Radical Jew: Paul and the Politics of Identity,* University of California Press, 1994.

> A *tour de force* of post-modern interpretation. Boyarin is a rabbi, a Talmud scholar who came to Paul in mid-life. He brings together a radical, post-Freudian re-interpretation of Paul with contemporary wrestlings over Zionism, feminism, and other fascinating topics.

*Bruce, F.F., *Paul: Apostle of the Heart Set Free,* Eerdmans, 1977.

A classic biography of Paul. Clear, well laid out, with all the details you wanted to know and lots you hadn't thought of before. Only faults: somewhat unexciting, and sometimes theologically naive.

Bultmann, Rudolf, *Theology of the New Testament,* translated by K. Grobel, 2 volumes, Scribner's, 1951–55.

Still enormously influential, though often at second-hand these days. Bultmann's treatment of Paul forms the major part of volume 1.

Dahl, N.A., *The Crucified Messiah and Other Essays,* Augsburg, 1974.
Dahl, N.A., *Studies in Paul: Theology for the Early Christian Mission,* Augsburg, 1977.

Dahl's two collections of essays are creative, innovative and thought-provoking. Though he interacts with the major schools of Pauline research, he is 'his own man' throughout.

Davies, W.D., *Paul and Rabbinic Judaism,* 4th edition, Fortress, 1980 [1948].

The fourth edition of Davies' classic work, which changed the direction of Pauline studies after the war.

Dictionary of Paul and his Letters, edited by Gerald F. Hawthorne, Ralph P. Martin, and Daniel G. Reid, InterVarsity Press, 1993.

A major recent tool. Conservative but not uncritically so.

Dunn, James D.G., *Christology in the Making: A New Testament Inquiry Into the Origins of the Doctrine of the Incarnation,* 2nd edition (1989), Eerdmans, 1996.

Dunn's famous treatment of Christology, in which Paul plays a central role. Few, however, have followed him in his conclusions at this point.

Dunn, James D.G., *Jesus, Paul and the Law: Studies in Mark and Galatians,* Westminster / John Knox, 1990.

A collection of articles, some of which have been of lasting importance in recent debate.

Fee, Gordon D., *God's Empowering Presence: The Holy Spirit in the Letters of Paul,* Hendrickson, 1994.

Over nine hundred packed pages: an exhaustive survey of what precisely Paul meant in every passage where he refers to the Spirit. A treasure-house.

Gaston, Lloyd, *Paul and the Torah,* University of British Columbia Press, 1987.

Gaston is a delightful maverick, who has tried to make out that Paul had nothing whatever against Judaism. Remarkable for its ingenuity rather than its persuasiveness, as witness the fact that few have followed his lead.

Gospel in Paul: Studies on Corinthians, Galatians and Romans for Richard N. Longenecker, edited by L. Ann Jervis and Peter Richardson, *Journal for the Study of the New Testament Supplement Series*, Sheffield Academic Press, 1994, no. 108.

A brand-new collection of articles by some major scholars.

Hays, R.B., *The Faith of Jesus Christ: An Investigation of the Narrative Substructure of Galatians 3:1 – 4:11,* S.B.L. Dissertation Series, Scholars Press, 1983.

Hays, R.B., *Echoes of Scripture in the Letters of Paul,* Yale University Press, 1989.

Hays has become a major force in Pauline studies. His second book is widely, and rightly, influential on both sides of the Atlantic. Reawakes the echoes of the Jewish Bible that scholars had ignored or forgotten in reading Paul.

Hengel, Martin, *The Pre-Christian Paul,* in collaboration with Roland Dienes, translated by John Bowden, Trinity Press International, 1991.

Hengel, probably the most learned New Testament scholar in the world today, investigates Paul's Jewish upbringing up to the time of his conversion. Very important.

*Hooker, Morna D., *Pauline Pieces,* Epworth Press, 1979.

A very useful, clear, and accessible introduction to Paul, by one of Britain's leading scholars.

Hooker, Morna D., *From Adam to Christ: Essays on Paul,* Cambridge University Press, 1990.

A collection of more scholarly, but still very clear and interesting, articles.

Käsemann, Ernst, *New Testament Questions of Today,* Fortress, 1969.

Käsemann, Ernst, *Perspectives on Paul*, translated by Margaret Kohl, Fortress, 1971 [1969].

Käsemann, Ernst, *Commentary on Romans,* Eerdmans, 1980 [1973].

Käsemann is the most exciting of the post-Bultmann generation of German scholars on Paul. Pre-Sanders, of course, but lots of material of abiding worth. Not an easy read, though, for the most part. His Romans commentary more than repays the effort.

Kim, Seyoon, *The Origin of Paul's Gospel,* Wissenschaftliche Untersuchungen zum neuen Testament 2, 2nd edition, J.C.B. Mohr (Paul Siebeck), 1984.

Kim argues in massive detail, often quite technically, that Paul's conversion, understood in a particular way, was the tap-root for his subsequent fully developed theology.

Maccoby, Hyam, *The Mythmaker: Paul and the Invention of Christianity,* Harper and Row, 1986.

Maccoby, Hyam, *Paul and Hellenism,* Trinity Press International, 1991.

Maccoby believes that Paul was a thoroughly Hellenized thinker who transformed the pure Jewish religion of Jesus into a corrupt and virtually pagan system, which became the origin of subsequent anti-Semitism. Not many scholars agree with him, but he's an influential spokesman for this point of view.

Malherbe, Abraham J., *Paul and the Popular Philosophers,* Fortress, 1989.

Malherbe is a leading American student of first-century popular philosophical movements. This book opens our eyes to see some of the parallels, and differences, between these movements and Paul which would have been quite obvious at the time.

McGrath, Alister E., *Iustitia Dei. A History of the Christian Doctrine of Justification,* 2 volumes, Cambridge University Press, 1986.

Everything about justification except its detailed basis – which, as McGrath recognizes, may not support what many have tried to build on it.

Meeks, Wayne A., *The First Urban Christians: The Social World of the Apostle Paul,* Yale University Press, 1983.

A major and important study, putting Paul and his congregations into their first-century social context.

Neill, Stephen: see under Wright, N.T.

Räisänen, Heikki, *Paul and the Law,* Fortress, 1986a [1983].

Räisänen, Heikki, *The Torah and Christ: Essays in German and English on the Problem of the Law in Early Christianity,* Suomen Ekseegeettisen Seuran Julkaisuja, Finnish Exegetical Society, 1986b.

Räisänen's views, though shrill (Paul, he says, is radically inconsistent about the law), are thoroughly well worked out, and he continues to be influential.

Ridderbos, Herman N., *Paul: An Outline of His Theology,* translated by J.R. de Witt, Eerdmans, 1975 [1966].

A major and solid work by a leading scholar. Though 'pre-Sanders', this book remains enormously useful for the serious reader of Paul.

Sanders, E.P., *Paul and Palestinian Judaism: A Comparison of Patterns of Religion,* Fortress, 1977.
Sanders, E.P., *Paul, the Law, and the Jewish People,* Fortress, 1983.
*Sanders, E.P., *Paul,* Past Masters, Oxford University Press, 1991.

The books that turned the tide. *Paul and Palestinian Judaism*, though massive, and in some ways curiously unsystematic and incomplete, remains central to subsequent study. *Paul, the Law, and the Jewish People* fills in some of the gaps about the law and the Jews. *Paul* is the little book that will start you off...

Schoeps, H.-J., *Paul: The Theology of the Apostle in the Light of Jewish Religious History,* translated by H. Knight, Westminster, 1961 [1959].

An earlier, more nuanced, moderate and scholarly version of Maccoby (see above).

Schweitzer, Albert, *Paul and His Interpreters: A Critical History,* translated by William Montgomery (1912), MacMillan, 1950.

A good read, as much for its light on Paul as on the critics, mostly (but not all) now forgotten, whom Schweitzer was categorizing and criticizing.

Schweitzer, Albert, *The Mysticism of Paul the Apostle,* translated by William Montgomery, Preface by F.C. Burkitt, Seabury Press, 1968 [1930].

The great book by the old master. Still well worth reading. Schweitzer saw the problems, and tried to solve them creatively, long before most others.

Segal, Alan F., *Paul the Convert: The Apostolate and Apostasy of Saul the Pharisee,* Yale University Press, 1990.

A far more interesting Jewish book on Paul than those of Maccoby. Segal is sympathetic to Paul, but his reading is still quite lop-sided.

*Stendahl, K., *Paul Among Jews and Gentiles,* Fortress, 1976.

Contains Stendahl's seminal essay on 'Paul and the Introspective Conscience of the West', which alerted the world to problems in traditional readings of Paul some while before Sanders. Other interesting material, too, all clearly presented and accessible to ordinary readers.

Theissen, Gerd, *The Social Setting of Pauline Christianity: Essays on Corinth,* Fortress, 1982.

Like Meeks (though not always so crystal clear), Theissen tries to set Paul and his churches in their sociological context.

Theissen, Gerd, *Psychological Aspects of Pauline Theology*, translated by John P. Galvin, Fortress, 1987 [1983].

A bit of a *tour de force*, and not always completely convincing. Fascinating attempt to understand Paul psychologically, with some creative bits of exegesis *en route*.

Thielman, Frank, *From Plight to Solution: A Jewish Framework for Understanding Paul's View of the Law in Galatians and Romans,* Supplements to Novum Testamentum, E.J. Brill, 1989.
Thielman, Frank, *Paul and the Law,* InterVarsity Press, 1995.

One of the best of the younger generation of Pauline scholars. Clear, refreshing, incisive, even when one may not agree.

*Wenham, David, *Paul: Follower of Jesus or Founder of Christianity?* Eerdmans, 1995.

The fullest, best and most recent study of the relationship between Jesus and Paul.

*Westerholm, Stephen, *Israel's Law and the Church's Faith: Paul and His Recent Interpreters,* Eerdmans, 1988.

An excellent introduction to contemporary Pauline studies, with a careful, measured and reasonable argument for a non-Sanders position on Paul and the law.

Wilson, A.N., *Paul: The Mind of the Apostle,* Norton, 1997.

Interesting and lively on the historical and cultural setting of Paul's work, with some suggestive ideas. Hopeless on theology: ignores the centrality, for Paul, of Jesus' resurrection, and supposes that his view of the cross was part psychological fixation, part derivation from the Mithras cult.

Witherington, Ben III, *Jesus, Paul and the End of the World: A Comparative Study in New Testament Eschatology*, InterVarsity Press, 1992.

Witherington, Ben III, *Paul's Narrative Thought World: The Tapestry of Tragedy and Triumph*, Westminster/John Knox, 1994.

Two substantial, but easy to read, treatments of Paul. Both will give much food for thought, though ultimately some may want to go further in various directions.

Wright, N.T., *The Epistles of Paul to the Colossians and to Philemon,* Tyndale Commentaries, Eerdmans, 1986.

Short accessible commentary, including detailed discussion of the significant poem of Colossians 1:15-20.

Wright, N.T. (with Stephen Neill), *The Interpretation of the New Testament, 1861–1986,* Oxford University Press, 1988.

Includes (pages 403–30) discussion of highlights of Pauline scholarship from Schweitzer to the 1980s.

Wright, N.T., *The Climax of the Covenant: Christ and the Law in Pauline Theology,* Fortress, 1991.

Collected exegetical essays on Paul's Christology and his view of the law. Lots of technical argument and Greek! Students report that they found the chapter on Romans 9–11 the most helpful thing they'd read on that much-debated section.

Wright, N.T., *The New Testament and the People of God,* Fortress, 1992.

Lays out the groundwork for study of early Christianity, Paul included. Particularly relevant to Paul is the discussion of the Pharisees and other aspects of second-temple Judaism (pages 181–203).

Wright, N.T., '"That we might become the righteousness of God": Reflections on 2 Corinthians 5:21', in *Pauline Theology,* edited by D.M. Hay, Fortress, 1993, volume II, pages 200–208.

Examines a key text for the 'righteousness of God' discussion.

Wright, N.T., 'Gospel and Theology in Galatians', in *Gospel in Paul: Studies on Corinthians, Galatians and Romans for Richard N. Longenecker,* edited by

L. Ann Jervis and Peter Richardson, *Journal for the Study of the New Testament*, Supplement Series, Sheffield Academic Press, 1994, no. 108, pages 222–39.

What did Paul mean by 'the gospel'?

Wright, N.T., 'Romans and Pauline Theology', in *Pauline Theology*, edited by David M. Hay and E. Elizabeth Johnson, Fortress, 1995, volume III, pages 30–67.

What makes Romans tick, theologically speaking? How does it *work*?

Wright, N.T., *Jesus and the Victory of God,* Fortress, 1996.

Not directly relevant to Paul, but extremely relevant to the question of whether Paul misunderstood Jesus!

Wright, N.T., 'Paul, Arabia and Elijah (Galatians 1:17)', in *Journal of Biblical Literature*, 1996, volume 115, pages 683–92.

Wright, N.T., 'The Law in Romans 2', in *Paul and the Mosaic Law*, edited by J.D.G. Dunn, J.C.B. Mohr (Paul Siebeck), 1996, pages 131–50.

*Ziesler, John A., *Pauline Christianity* (revised edition), The Oxford Bible Series, Oxford University Press, 1990 [1983].

A splendid short survey of Paul's thought, accessible and clear.